Set design by Peter Harrison

Photo by Robert Clayton

(Left to right) Sam Stewart, Craig Bockhorn, Anderson Matthews and Joyce Cohen in the Salt Lake City production of *Laughing Stock*.

LAUGHING STOCK

BY CHARLES MOREY

DRAMATISTS
PLAY SERVICE
INC.

LAUGHING STOCK
Copyright © 2006, Charles Morey

All Rights Reserved

SPECIAL NOTE

SPECIAL NOTE ON MUSIC

Dedicated to the memory of
Sally Stearns Brown, 1914–1983.

AUTHOR'S NOTE

Laughing Stock is essentially a farce and most of these characters are types we all know (and perhaps even love). However, it is of great importance that productions avoid the temptation to push these stereotypes too broadly. At the end of both acts the play turns towards a distinctly gentler comic tone. In order to navigate that turn successfully, the characters must be portrayed as real people with real concerns for whom we have empathy. Also, the comic engine of the play will not function properly if they are portrayed as woefully inept. In some cases they simply lack experience; in others, they are guilty of serious lapses of judgment and/or taste, to be sure, but they are not incapable. They are, for the most part, well intentioned individuals over-matched by circumstances and perhaps a series of ill-advised choices. The humor derives not from the disasters that befall them, but the manner in which they attempt to cope with those disasters, cover their miscues and right the sinking ship.

The setting should suggest the classic New England, post and beam, barn theatre. *Laughing Stock* has been variously designed for proscenium stages with the "Playhouse stage" directly up center or set to one side with the ability to jackknife into a position flat on to the audience for the performance scenes. It is helpful, but not essential, if the "Playhouse stage" can be closed off by a curtain. The one location outside the barn — the New York audition studio — can be suggested by lights alone or very minimal scenery. Thrust or arena stagings may, by necessity, take different approaches to the scenic design.

The inspiration for this play is a very real place. It doesn't exist anymore. Oh, the theatre itself still exists and, in fact, thrives, but has grown as an institution and physical plant far beyond the fictional "Playhouse" I depict in *Laughing Stock*. The theatre I remember was the classic New England barn. It served as performing space, rehearsal hall and scene shop rolled into one. There was no air-conditioning. Big barn doors with screens provided the only ventilation and served as minimal protection against omnipresent mosquitoes the size of sparrows. The dressing rooms were in the old cow tie-up; the box office and business office in the wood shed. It accommodated one hundred and forty-nine patrons on uncomfortable folding chairs. But despite meager resources, when everybody worked together to tell a story honestly at its simplest level — and the temperature-humidity index and the mosquitoes cooperated — there was work of which we were often proud.

Everyone in the theatre has their own "Playhouse." The place where there was never enough of anything: time, staff, money, and sometimes simply not enough talent or skill; where sometimes the doors fell off their hinges, the sound cues ran backwards and the occasional entrance was missed — but where you gave yourself over wholly to the making of plays, to telling stories in the dark on a summer night — and along the way made a little family as well for a few months. It is those places, and especially those people, this play celebrates. I hope what finally comes through *Laughing Stock* is a genuine affection and respect for those mostly honorable and sometimes inspired fools who inhabit this profession.

—Charles Morey, 2005

LAUGHING STOCK was originally produced by the Pioneer Theatre Company (Charles Morey, Artistic Director; Chris Lino Managing Director) in Salt Lake City, Utah, opening on February 7, 2001. It was directed by Charles Morey; the set design was by Peter Harrison; the costume design was by K.L. Alberts; the lighting design was by Karl E. Haas; the sound design was by Joe Payne; the original music was by James Prigmore; the production stage manager was John W. Caywood, Jr.; and the assistant stage manager was Erin Coffey. The cast was as follows:

GORDON PAGE	Anderson Matthews
JACK MORRIS	Robert J. Hamilton
SUSANNAH HUNTSMEN	Anne Stewart Mark
MARY PIERRE	Julie-Anne Leichty
TYLER TAYLOR	Kaleo Griffith
VERNON VOLKER	Max Robinson
RICHFIELD HAWKSLEY	Richard Mathews
DAISY COATES	Patricia Fraser
CRAIG CONLIN	Craig Bockhorn
SARAH MCKAY	Joyce Cohen
HENRY MILLS	Sam Stewart
BRAUN OAKES	Joshua Biton
KARMA SCHNEIDER	Tammy Leigh Davis
IAN MILLIKEN	Stephen Ivey

CHARACTERS

GORDON PAGE, artistic director (40s)

JACK MORRIS, an actor (20s)

SUSANNAH HUNTSMEN, a director (30s)

MARY PIERRE, an actress (20s)

TYLER TAYLOR, an actor (30s)

VERNON VOLKER, an actor (50s)

RICHFIELD HAWKSLEY, an actor (70s)

DAISY COATES, an actress (60s)

CRAIG CONLIN, managing director (40s)

SARAH MCKAY, stage manager (40s)

HENRY MILLS, a designer (30s)

KARMA SCHNEIDER, an apprentice

BRAUN OAKES, an apprentice

IAN MILLIKEN, an apprentice

SETTING

The action of the play takes place in and around the New England summer stock barn theatre known as "The Playhouse" and various other suggested locations from February to Labor Day of a recent year.

NOTES

If the technology is unavailable or should local fire laws prohibit the "exploding cross," the moment may be played as if the cross were intended to explode on cue but (of course) malfunctioned.

LAUGHING STOCK

ACT ONE

Scene 1

February. In the darkness, the beam of a flashlight cutting across indeterminate clutter.

JACK. Jeez, it's cold!
GORDON. I know. I just have to find the master. *(The flashlight goes out.)* Damn! These things never work. *(A crash.)* OW!!!
JACK. You OK?
GORDON. Yeah. *(He strikes a match.)* Here it is … I've got it. *(The match goes out.)* Ow! *(He exits. A mechanical click and a wildly cluttered space is dimly illuminated. He re-enters.)* This is it!
JACK. This is it?
GORDON. Yep. This is it.
JACK. Well … uh … wow!
GORDON. Yeah. It's a barn.
JACK. No. I mean yeah. It really is a barn.
GORDON. The cows walked out and the actors walked in.
JACK. When?
GORDON. Well, not actually. I mean cows did walk out. They're not still here. But they did have cows in here, oh, over, one, two hun … well lots of years ago. In the dressing rooms, when it rains, two centuries worth of cow shit … phew! They renovated it in '33. That's when our theatre started.
JACK. Renovated it? Where?
GORDON. Well, the stage — they put in the stage.
JACK. Is this like a snipe hunt? So, come on, really. Where's the theatre. This is the scene shop, right?

GORDON. Well ... yes. We build scenery here too. But this is the theatre.

JACK. Where does the audience sit?

GORDON. Here. Right here where we're standing.

JACK. You have seats?

GORDON. Of course. Over there. Folded up.

JACK. Folding chairs. Metal folding chairs.

GORDON. Keeps 'em awake. No snoring during *Peer Gynt*.

JACK. You did *Peer Gynt*?

GORDON. Last year. So, what do you think? I know it's rustic.

JACK. Rustic may be an understatement.

GORDON. But it really is charming — has loads of charm when it's cleaned up. I'd like you to be a part of it.

JACK. Well ... uh ... great. What's the season?

GORDON. *Dracula* ...

JACK. Which one, the Balderston and ...

GORDON. New adaptation. Very faithful to the novel.

JACK. Whose?

GORDON. My own ... *Dracul, Prince of the Undead*. No royalties.

JACK. I look forward to reading it.

GORDON. So do I. I mean it's almost ... not quite ... yet. And then *Charley's Aunt* and *Lear*.

JACK. *Lear*! Here?

GORDON. "Howl, howl, howl ... "

JACK. That's awfully big for a theatre like this isn't it?

GORDON. We're cutting it down of course. Very lean, spare production. Lots of doubling and tripling, loads of theatricality. That's one of the reasons we're trying rep.

JACK. Rep?

GORDON. Yep. Small, tight, talented company doing three great plays. One night *Dracula*, the next *Charley's Aunt* and *Lear* in between for the matinee.

JACK. Certainly cold enough in here for the heath ... Is there heat? Or air in the summer I mean?

GORDON. Only what nature provides through those big barn doors. "Blow winds, and crack your cheeks! Rage, blow! ... "

JACK. Who's playing Lear?

GORDON. I am. It's time for me to tackle that son of a bitch. Run a summer theatre for twelve years and you'll understand. You wouldn't believe the local critics. "How sharper than a serpent's tooth ... "

10

JACK. I thought he was referring to his daughters.

GORDON. Whose?

JACK. Lear's.

GORDON. Oh! Right. Of course.

JACK. Who's directing?

GORDON. I am.

JACK. You are?

GORDON. I know. But it's my time to tackle the son of a bitch. What the hell.

JACK. Yeah. What the hell.

GORDON. Listen. You could do ... what's his name?

JACK. Edmund?

GORDON. What? No. In *Dracula*. You could do ... what's his name?

JACK. Renfield?

GORDON. No, I'm cutting him, the other one ...

JACK. Well, I'd love to try him ...

GORDON. No, no. I don't mean Dracul ... I see him very ... But, you know, the one who always says, "But surely, Dr. Van Helsing, you can't mean there are such things as vampires!"

JACK. Oh, yeah. Well ...

GORDON. And then Edmund or Edgar. Which one is the bastard? I can never keep them straight.

JACK. Good thing you're not playing Gloucester.

GORDON. Why?

JACK. He's their father.

GORDON. Right! Yes. Of course.

JACK. Who is playing Gloucester? Or anything else?

GORDON. Richfield Hawksley will play Gloucester. He's been with us forever. Started here as an apprentice when Maria Ouspenskya was the artistic director. He was Jimmy Stewart's roommate at Princeton.

JACK. Good Lord, he must be ninety ...

GORDON. No. Not ninety.

JACK. I mean if he was Jimmy Stewart's roommate?

GORDON. Maybe it was Stewart Granger. Anyway he's still sharp as a ... well, great stories. I don't know how the rest of the company will fall out yet, some old, some new. And *Charley's Aunt*. Ever done it?

JACK. No, but I've wanted to. It is a very funny play. One of the great farces.

GORDON. Four times. Wore the dress once.

JACK. Are you directing that too?

GORDON. No. Susannah Huntsmen. Do you know her? Very sharp. Right out of Yale. Her first professional gig, but she has some extraordinary ideas.

JACK. About *Charley's Aunt*?

GORDON. She did this amazing thesis project on Noel Coward in the Yale swimming pool. Puppets. Gender switching. Synchronized … very erotic.

JACK. You saw this?

GORDON. She wrote Barbara about it.

JACK. Barbara?

GORDON. Barbara DeMartineau. Our major donor. Without her annual donation the Playhouse couldn't make it. Barbara's very strong on encouraging young directors — particularly women — and particularly women who are daughters of her roommate at Vassar. She lives in Palm Beach in the winter.

JACK. Susannah?

GORDON. Barbara.

JACK. Oh … So, *Charley's Aunt*?

GORDON. You know, to be frank, and I'm not putting you on, I think you could wear the dress.

JACK. Really?

GORDON. Would you want to?

JACK. Well, it's one of the funniest …

GORDON. Some guys are very … well particularly straight guys … they're nervous about … You are aren't you?

JACK. Last I checked.

GORDON. Good. I was afraid I might have put my foot in it there. I mean it would be OK if you weren't …

JACK. I am.

GORDON. You are?

JACK. No. I'm not. I'm …

GORDON. That's good. I didn't mean "that's good that you're not." I mean that's good that … that … so, you'd be OK with the dress?

JACK. It's one of the funniest parts ever written. I'd love to play it some time.

GORDON. Good! Well, it's done then … OK?

JACK. Well, I, uh … I don't know whether I should really leave town, now. My agent won't want me to, I'm sure. I'm just starting to get sent out for commercials, a first refusal last week, in fact, and I've had a callback for *All My Children*.

GORDON. Oh. Good.

JACK. And it's still pilot season and you never know what might …

GORDON. Oh, I know.

JACK. And it is four months away.

GORDON. You'll think about it. Thank you for coming up anyway and auditioning.

JACK. Sure. No. Thank you. For the offer. We'll just have to see …

GORDON. Shall we go back to the farmhouse…?

JACK. Yeah. It is really cold.

GORDON. It's February. I'll get the ghost light this time so we don't kill ourselves. *(He exits, turns off the lights. The stage is plunged into darkness momentarily, then the ghost light comes up slowly on dimmer, bathing the barn in a warm and theatrical amber.)* I know what it looks like now. But come summer, July, a beautiful New England evening, the sun setting "back of our mountain" like Mr. Wilder says … And sometimes the sunset slants across the roof, through the sugar maples, and catches the screens in those big barn doors with a lighting effect you could only dream about recreating on a stage. And other times the evening light is so clear it makes everything stand out like an impressionist painting … crickets … and then, a couple of hundred people come *here* to sit in the dark on uncomfortable chairs in a two-hundred-year-old barn with no air-conditioning to watch us act out stories. Why? It's a complete mystery to me. A miracle of sorts. Who could not want to be a part of that? *(Lights change. Jack exits. Gordon remains.)*

Scene 2

Susannah joins him. They set up a table and chairs to represent a New York audition studio. The apprentices clear the barn during the transition.

MARY. *(Entering.)* Hi!

GORDON. Hi.

MARY. I'm Mary. Thanks so much for seeing me. I have really,

really wanted to audition for you for like ever. How long are you in New York, anyway? 'Cause if you're here this weekend I'm doing a showcase. Theatro Grosso in the Bronx. It's right on the D train past Yankee Stadium. Here's a flyer. It's a new adaption of the *Epic of Gilgamesh*, you know like Persia or Iran or something back like before the Middle Ages even — though I don't know if there's an old adaption even — I get raped by the gods. Can you believe it?

GORDON. Raped by the gods? Really?

MARY. Yeah. I hate it when that happens. But I offer myself, really … like as a virginal sacrifice? Kevin's working on that with me. Kevin's directing. And he wrote it. Like the adaptation. Not the original epic. I think that was Eugene O'Neill or Lope de Vega or somebody. Am I talking too much? I'm going to do Ophelia. 'Kay? Do you mind if I use you?

GORDON. No, I don't. Susannah?

SUSANNAH. Don't use me. I don't like to be used.

MARY. Could you sit like there? *(Indicating for Gordon to move his chair to the side of the table.)*

GORDON. Susannah's directing *Charley's Aunt*.

MARY. Cool. *(Shaking out.)* I am so tense. *(Rolling her head.)* Ohhh … Ohhh … Ohhhh … *(Suddenly.)* "There's fennel for you, and columbines. There's rue for you and here's some for me. We may call it herb of Grace o'Sundays. O you must wear your rue with a difference. There's a daisy. I would give you some violets, but they withered all when my father died. They say he made a good end." *(Sings.)*

And will he not come again?
And will he not come again?
No, no he is dead;
Go to thy deathbed;
He never will come again.

(By the end of the song she has managed to drape herself across Gordon.)

GORDON. Ummm … well … Good. Good. Interesting choice.

MARY. I think she's offering herself to Claudius, I really do. I'm working on her in class.

GORDON. Really?

MARY. Paul, my teacher, says my work lacks emotional intimacy.

GORDON. Really?

MARY. Yeah. But I'm really trying to open myself more to opening my intimacy in my emotional work.

GORDON. Good. Really.

MARY. This piece has never been that full for me before.

GORDON. Really? Good.

MARY. Need any more?

GORDON. Well, I don't need any more … need to see any more … I think that'll do me … do it … for today … Susannah? *(Mary bends over to pick up her bag.) Charley's Ass?* AUNT! *(Mary starts to leave.)*

MARY. 'Kay! Thanks!

SUSANNAH. Oh, Mary? Do you swim? *(Lights change. Mary exits. Tyler enters.)*

TYLER. *(Reading from the manuscript.)* "You fools! Pitiful fools! You shall tear each your eyes out yet in fear and horror of me, Dracul, Prince of the Undead! You think you have left me without a place to rest but I have one last box. Search as you will, you shall never find me. I shall sleep in my earth box for centuries. My revenge has just begun. Hear my prophecy!"

GORDON. Good. Good! Good!!! Tyler. Tell me. You've done this before?

TYLER. Last winter. The Art Factory Dinner Playhouse. We used the old script though … creaks, I want to tell you. This text. Yours…?

GORDON. I'm trying to do the novel justice.

TYLER. Well, that's what I'd like to do. Do Dracula, Vlad the Impaler, justice. Boy would that be refreshing. Is there a second act?

GORDON. Coming … very close … it's all … *(He taps his head.)*

TYLER. Well, if it's anything like this, you are home free, man. I need to do him again, you know. At the Art Factory it was all so surface … cape and smoke and teeth and prime rib if you know what I mean. I hate all those cheap tricks. I want to find my inner Vlad the Impaler.

GORDON. Well, your inner … in that … I mean it spoke … So you'd be interested in coming back? After last summer? I mean *Peer Gynt* and the flying pig and all?

TYLER. Hey, I love it up there, man, that barn. And I won't trivialize Vlad. I will live him for you, man. If you can live the undead, if you know what I mean.

GORDON. That's terrific, Tyler. Thanks … Oh, Tyler, by the way, did you, by any chance, keep the cape and the teeth?

TYLER. Of course. *(Lights change. Tyler exits. Vernon enters.)*

VERNON. This is the Playhouse audition…?

GORDON. Yes, yes. Come in. You're…?

VERNON. So. I'm here to "audition" my agent tells me.

15

GORDON. Yes. I'm Gordon Page, Artistic Director. My Guest Director, Susannah Huntsmen ... uh ... do you have a picture and resume? I don't think I've got one here.

VERNON. My agent didn't send it over?

GORDON. Doesn't look like it.

VERNON. I don't believe it. That hack. I don't know if I've got one here. *(Casually searches his briefcase.)* Don't use them much any more.

GORDON. Really?

VERNON. Most people in the business know me. Thirty years and I guess you still need a picture and resume.

GORDON. Well, it's a formality really, but ...

VERNON. Who's playing Lear?

GORDON. Me.

VERNON. Of course.

GORDON. My time to tackle the son ...

VERNON. I did it with Joe in the park. The early days, before he started screwing around with movie stars. Have we met before?

GORDON. I don't know we may have, I'm Gordon Page ...

VERNON. I don't think we've met. Tell me about your theatre.

GORDON. Well, we're an old, old summer theatre. It's a barn ...

VERNON. I did that circuit. Ogunquit. Kennebunkport. Lakes Region, the Cape. When they did plays. Before it was all *Nunsense 5* and the *Plaid* thing with aging adolescents from the *Brady Bunch*.

GORDON. Well, we do plays, no musicals.

VERNON. That's why I'm here. I'll do Gloucester for you, Van Helsing, and whatever you want in that stupid farce. You can take that load off your mind.

GORDON. Well ... Van Helsing and Gloucester are cast, Richfield Hawksley, but would you mind taking a look at Cornwall? *(Offering him a script.)*

VERNON. Cornwall? ... The light in here is pretty bad ...

GORDON. You could do something from memory.

VERNON. A monologue? A memorized speech? Like in school?

GORDON. Well, I mean, if the light ...

VERNON. Like "Now is the winter of our discontent ... " or "This is an important part of Grover's Corners ... " Call the agent. Tell him to set it up. But my time is kind of tight today. Very nice to meet you. Don't get up. *(He turns to leave.)*

SUSANNAH. *(In a loud whisper.)* He is perfect! I love his energy!

GORDON. What's his name? *(Vernon exits. Lights change. Susannah exits as Gordon makes a call on his cell phone.)*

GORDON. Barbara? ... Mrs. DeMartineau? This is Gordon Page ... from the Playhouse. Yes ... That's right ... *Peer Gynt* it was called ... Those were trolls. Ha, ha ... Oh ... well, I am sorry ... *Sound of Music*? ... Well, I don't think we could fit the Alps in the barn, ha, ha ... Those were fjords in *Peer Gynt* ... fjords ... fjords ... no, not Fiji ... FEE-YORDS! Fiji is in the South Pacific ... Yes. Yes, I have seen that one. It is a good one. "Bali Hi" to you too. Well, actually, we were wondering ... you see, we haven't received your annual very generous, uh, check ... Ah ... Oh ... I see. *Peer Gynt* ... You really feel that? ... I see ... No, we will never do it again ... Or anything by Ibsen again ... Or anything like it was by Ibsen again. Really. I promise. Never again ... Thank you, Mrs. DeMartineau, thank you ... Oh, this year? *Dracula, Charley's Aunt* and *King Lear* ... It's not really that depressing ... ultimately very uplifting ... lots of uplift ... No, no, I suppose it's never too late to change ... Any Shakespeare other than *King Lear*? But! ... I see ... Yes, I do understand. We do need your support. Thank you, Mrs. DeMartineau, we appreciate ... Mrs. DeMartineau? Mrs. DeMartineau? *(Richfield and Daisy enter.)*

RICHFIELD. Gordon!

GORDON. Richfield! Daisy? What are you doing here ... not to audition certainly.

RICHFIELD. Good God, I hope not.

DAISY. We met for coffee. Thought we'd drop by ...

RICHFIELD. ... drop by since you were in town. How's my wonderful old barn, my temple among the elms, doing under its wintery blanket?

GORDON. Well, it's May ...

RICHFIELD. *(To Susannah, who is re-entering.)* Richfield Hawksley ...

GORDON. Oh, sorry, Richfield, Susannah Huntsmen. Susannah, Daisy Coates. Richfield and Daisy have been in the company since ... forever. Susannah's directing *Charley's Aunt*.

DAISY. How wonderful.

GORDON. And she'll be doing a bit of acting, too. Barbara wanted her to have the experience. Seems she's never been on stage. *(A nervous laugh.)*

RICHFIELD. Really?

SUSANNAH. I don't think directing has anything to do with acting.

DAISY. Really?

RICHFIELD. Did *Charley's Aunt* at the Playhouse in '48. Again

17

in … whenever … when this lad put on the dress.

SUSANNAH. What dress?

RICHFIELD. What dress?! Good! Haha! Good!

GORDON. Good. Yes. What dress? … My God.

RICHFIELD. Tell me what year you were born and I'll tell you what plays we were doing in that wonderful old barn among the sugar maples.

SUSANNAH. What plays you do doesn't matter. It's what you do *to* them. ⚥

GORDON. Well, not …

RICHFIELD. Exactly! Madame Ouspenskya used to say to me when I was even younger than you are … she used to say … well, I can't remember what she used to say. But, Gordon, I want you to know, I have learned it. Letter-perfect. I have learned it.

DAISY. He's been working on it all year.

RICHFIELD. A solid year, by God, but I learned it! "As flies to wanton boys are we to the gods, they kill us for their sport."

GORDON. Oh shit.

RICHFIELD. *(To Susannah.)* King Lear. The Earl of Gloucester. Blind you know by this point.

GORDON. Richfield. We've changed the schedule. We're doing … "Hamlet."

RICHFIELD. We're not doing *Lear* anymore?

DAISY. It's *Hamlet* now?

RICHFIELD. Why?

GORDON. Barbara thinks *Lear* is too depressing. Besides, it's my time to tackle the son of a bitch, Richfield, it's my time. And we've got a fabulous Ophelia …

DAISY. You've already got your Ophelia?

GORDON. Yes. Uh. Daisy, I thought maybe Gertrude?

DAISY. Whatever.

GORDON. "What a rogue and peasant slave I am … "

RICHFIELD. "Am I … "

GORDON. "Am I … "

RICHFIELD. Oh shit. *(Lights change.)*

Scene 3

*The company enter, set up chairs, strike the audition table
and take their place in a loose horseshoe around the barn.
Gordon consults his notes then turns to the company.*

GORDON. Let me see … What's next?

SARAH. Cocktails!?

GORDON. Not yet … Not yet … Uh … Craig! It's up to you
now. Craig is our … What? What is your title now, you've taken
on so much …

CRAIG. Producing Executive Administrative Director.

GORDON. So … bathrooms, budgets and books? Does that sound
about right? Be nice to him. He fills the toilet paper dispensers and
writes the checks. *(An appreciative chuckle.)* But I sign them.

CRAIG. Very humorous Gordon, per usual. Well. I don't have to
tell you how happy I am you're all here. I stay up here all winter while
Gordon does artistic things in lofts and basements around New York.
And it's been a long winter. It's always a long winter. My job is to
keep all of you people organized, so if you'll follow the few simple
rules in these guidelines, *(He passes around some thick and impressive
looking handouts.)* we'll get through this summer … fine. *(Sits.)*

GORDON. That's it? … Nothing else? … OK, well …

CRAIG. *(Rises.)* I do want to add one thought. On the subject of
office supplies … *(A stifled laugh from Sarah.)* Now, I work in an
office. So I have office supplies. Most of you don't work in an
office, you work in … rehearsals … or someplace. So you don't
have office supplies. Now, I understand that. If you had an office,
you would have office supplies. But you don't. However, simply
because you don't have an office and therefore don't have office
supplies, this doesn't mean that my office supplies are therefore
your office supplies, even though they are the Playhouse office supplies, supplied by the Playhouse I mean and you are employed by
the Playhouse and therefore might assume you have a right to those
office supplies. You don't. Not my office supplies. I mean I am a
person, I have pencils. You are people too, so you should have pencils. But you don't. I don't know why you don't. I have pencils. I

take care of my pencils. I sharpen them. But you don't. You never seem to sharpen them. Why? I don't know. Probably because you don't have them. So why don't I ever have any pencils? When Henry comes in with the receipt for ten yards of fabric for fjords and I want to write that down in my account book I can't be looking all over for a pencil can I? I ask you? Can I? So. I hope we're clear on the subject of office supplies. I'm sure you will all have a wonderful and fulfilling summer here at the Playhouse and if you need anything …

RICHFIELD. … except pencils …

CRAIG. … stop into my office in the woodshed. *(He sits.)*

GORDON. Thanks, Craig, I'm sure …

SARAH. Craig? I have a question? *(He stands.)* What is the proper procedure, the correct protocol as it were, to get our money back if the Coke machine just eats it and we don't get a Coke? *(Guffaws from Richfield, Henry, Gordon and Tyler.)*

VERNON. *(To Jack.)* What the hell is that about?

CRAIG. The Coke machine! Gordon, I am not responsible … this summer I am not having anything to do with the Coca-Cola Bottling Company of Northern New England or any of their products. That machine is an abomination, it is a nightmare, it is my cross … *(Sarah vainly attempts to stifle her laughter.)* I am glad you find this funny, Sarah, I am glad you do, because I most certainly do not!

GORDON. Well, enough said about office supplies, pencils and Coca-Cola products. So — once again — welcome … It's going to be a … terrific … a wonderful … a great summer. And one word of wisdom for us all. "Speak the speech … " Oh, oh, I forgot. Mrs. DeMartineau sends her best to you all — and especially you Susannah — from Palm Beach … "Speak the speech … " Oh, and don't let me forget to introduce our hard-working apprentices, Karma, Ian, and Brown …

BRAUN. Braun.

GORDON. Brown.

BRAUN. Braun.

GORDON. … "Speak the speech trippingly, I pray you … Suit the movements to the actions and the actions to the movements … to hold, as if, a mirror up to nature … "

VERNON. *(A barely disguised groan.)* Good God …

GORDON. Now, there's beer and wine on the props table … *(The company move towards the refreshments.)* Oh! And, soft drinks

... soft drinks, too, Sarah. So, let's ... uh ... let's ... let's get to know one another and find out "What a piece of work is man."

VERNON. Is he always like that?

JACK. Like what?

VERNON. Well, misquoting everything and I mean just being an ...

JACK. I don't know. I only met him once. He seems sincere.

VERNON. Sincere? Yes, I suppose you could say that.

HENRY. *(Approaching Gordon, a script in hand. Craig joins them.)* Gordon, This *Dracul, Prince of the Undead* opus you just handed to your longtime designer, friend, and colleague for the very first time today on the eve of the first rehearsal ...

GORDON. Give it a chance, Henry I think you'll see ...

HENRY. Oh, I see already, Gordon. I see twenty sets, flying vampire bats, exploding crosses, chemical fog, wireless microphones, *(Exploding.)* not to mention *Charley's Aunt* and *Hamlet* in rotating rep on a stage the size of a comfortable walk-in closet!

GORDON. Henry, think theatrical and spare ... think theatrically spare ... Think fabric draped artistically here and there.

HENRY. I'm thinking disaster.

CRAIG. I'm thinking expensive.

GORDON. I'm thinking fabric ... draped artistically and economically here and there.

HENRY. And what about the budget this year?

CRAIG. You didn't tell him?

HENRY. Tell me what?

GORDON. A little less.

HENRY. Less?!

CRAIG. A fifteen percent cut.

HENRY. Gordon! Craig!

GORDON. Henry, you know last year was tough ...

CRAIG, GORDON and HENRY. *Peer Gynt.*

GORDON. ... just didn't sell.

CRAIG. And if we don't at least break even this year, we're in real trouble.

HENRY. You know I could have that job tomorrow if I wanted in the window dressing department at Macy's!

GORDON. Give it a chance, Henry. Just think one night *Dracula*, the next *Charley's Aunt* and *Hamlet* in between for the matinee. What a treat!

HENRY and CRAIG. For whom?

21

TYLER. Mary? Tyler Taylor. Wanted to say hey. You'll be my Mina, huh?

MARY. Right. You're Dracula? Wow. Are you going to have like the teeth and everything?

TYLER. Everything.

MARY. Wow.

TYLER. But it's the inner Vlad that really interests me, Mary.

MARY. Wow.

TYLER. Because the question is — what does it mean to be truly undead?

MARY. I think Mina really offers herself to him, don't you? Like a virginal sacrifice?

TYLER. That's really insightful. Do you want a glass of wine? *(Tyler places a protective arm about her shoulder and escorts her towards the refreshments.)*

RICHFIELD. Gordon?

GORDON. Yes, Richfield?

RICHFIELD. About your script of Dracula …

GORDON. *Dracul, Prince of the Undead.*

RICHFIELD. Yes, of course, *Dracul.* I think it's marvelous what you've done.

GORDON. Thank you.

RICHFIELD. You know I've done Van Helsing five times …

GORDON. That's why I cast you. Should come back to you pretty quickly.

RICHFIELD. Well, that's just it. You see in the version I've done there were two ingenues, Lucy Westenra and Mina Murray and you've only got Mina …

GORDON. Economy — both artistic and financial …

RICHFIELD. Of course, but in the other version there are three young men, Arthur Holmwood, Jonathan Harker, and Jack Seward. But you've got Seward as Mina's father so she's now Mina Seward and Harker is her fiancé and Lucy and Arthur aren't in it at all and well, I'm having a terrible time with the names.

GORDON. You'll be wonderful Richfield. You always are. You've done it five times. Piece of cake. *(Leaving Richfield.)*

SARAH. *(Passing in front of Gordon.)* Good welcome, Gordon. Craig was in fine form.

GORDON. Same old … is that…?

SARAH. Yes. Gordon. It is. A gin and tonic. A refreshing summer drink.

GORDON. Sarah …

SARAH. And I don't want to hear about it. *(She walks away.)*

GORDON. Sarah … *(Gordon follows her.)*

VERNON. Do you believe this place?

JACK. It's rustic, I guess?

VERNON. Rustic? Judy and Mickey meet the Joads. *(He goes to refill his empty glass.)*

RICHFIELD. Yes … *(Holding forth to the three apprentices.)* Started here with Ouspenskya. She was a disciple of Stanislavski, you know, at the Moscow Art Theatre. I trod these old boards with Kit Cornell, Helen Hayes …

DAISY. Alfred Lunt …

RICHFIELD. Lynn Fontaine …

KARMA. So like have there ever been any stars here?

VERNON. *(Having found his way to Susannah. Jack eases over to join them.)* I'll warn you up front. I don't do shtick.

SUSANNAH. Good.

VERNON. This farce shit doesn't interest me.

SUSANNAH. I don't think *Charley's Aunt* is a farce. *(She crosses away.)*

JACK. What did she say?

VERNON. This could be more interesting than I thought.

DAISY. Thornton Wilder was here, you know.

RICHFIELD. In *Our Town* I did Howie right there on that stage with Thornton Wilder as the Stage Manager …

IAN. Is Howie here this summer?

SUSANNAH. So, Mary, I want to ask you about this *Epic of Gilgamesh* you were in. I did my own all-female adaptation for my senior thesis at Sarah Lawrence …

TYLER. Excuse me, I was just getting her some more wine. You see the thing about playing Vlad, Mary, is to always remember that he is the Impaler …

GORDON. *(Finding his way to Jack.)* Jack, I am really pleased … and surprised actually that you joined us for the season. You know, I didn't think you would.

JACK. Well, to tell you the truth … well, it seemed like a good place to spend a summer.

GORDON. You'll enjoy it. I know you will. And you will be hysterical in *Charley's Aunt*.

JACK. You know, I just heard Susannah say something that …

SARAH. *(Loudly.)* So I told them at the clinic they could take

23

Betty and her Ford and put 'em where the moon don't shine …

GORDON. Oh God. Excuse me, Jack. Gotta go.

VERNON. OK. Tell me the truth. Why are you here? "It seemed like a good place to spend the summer." I know truthful acting when I see it and that wasn't.

JACK. Well, I wasn't going to accept the job. But I went back to New York and spent the whole winter and spring out of work without hardly an audition even and it all seemed so pointless, this "acting" stuff. And so, almost on a whim, I applied to Columbia Law School — and to my amazement — they accepted me. I start in September, but I still had this offer for the summer, so …

VERNON. Leaving the business? If only I'd had the brains thirty years ago.

JACK. Maybe we'll have some fun this summer.

VERNON. "Fun"? Sure. Fifty-five years old, thirty years in the business and I'm ready for some "fun" here in the mosquito capital of New England. *(Lights change.)*

Scene 4

The company rearranges the barn for the rehearsal of Dracul, Prince of the Undead.

DAISY, SUSANNAH and KARMA. *(As Transylvanian peasants.)* "Vrolak, Pokol, Ordog, vlokoslak, ordog … "

GORDON. OK! OK! Good. That's a good start. Let's move on. In the few minutes we have left let's jump into your first scene, Tyler, and see if we can't just throw it up on its feet … just breeze right through.

TYLER. Love to. Raring to go here.

GORDON. So, the peasants finish chanting "Vrolak, Pokol, Ordog … "

DAISY. You'll tell us what that means, sometime, won't you, Gordon?

GORDON. Of course. And Tyler, you're … when the lights change you're … hereish … and Jack you're still about thereish, OK? … and "Welcome to my … "

24

TYLER. Gordon.
GORDON. Yes.
TYLER. Sorry for stopping.
SARAH. And before we've even started.
GORDON. Not at all.
TYLER. How do I get here?
GORDON. What do you mean?
TYLER. I mean how do I get here?
GORDON. Ummm … Walk?
TYLER. In light? In the dark? Am I discovered?
GORDON. In light.
TYLER. Thanks.
GORDON. Good. So …
TYLER. And what's my "as if"?
GORDON. As if?
TYLER. As if I've come from…?
GORDON. As if you've come from your front door?
TYLER. That's what I thought.
GORDON. OK. Good. Tyler, you enter as if coming from your front door … "Welcome, welcome … "
TYLER. Have you thought about morphing?
GORDON. Morphing?
TYLER. What if I morphed …
SARAH. Morphed?
TYLER. … morphed from my bat-form, or possibly my wolf-form … into my human form.
MARY. Oh. Wow.
SARAH. And how does one morph?
TYLER. Acting, Sarah. Acting.
SARAH. Oh … acting.
GORDON. Tyler, I don't know if …
TYLER. Let me show you, Gordon. Just let me show you. Now I haven't worked on this. It's not fully internalized yet, and it would need music …
SARAH. I'll hum something from *Jekyll and Hyde*.
TYLER. But this is kind of the idea. *(He curls himself into a ball on the floor and through an extended series of grunts and postures "transforms" himself from a "wolf" into human form.)* "Welcome to my house, Mr. Harker, enter freely" … etc., etc. What do you think?
SARAH. Was that the bat or the wolf?
TYLER. Gordon …

JACK. But if I see him morph…?

TYLER. Gordon?

JACK. Why would I go into the house with him if I've seen him morph?

TYLER. That would become your actor's task to justify …

JACK. … to justify how dumb Harker is to sit down to dinner with someone he's just seen morph from a bat?

TYLER. That was a wolf, but, if you want me to suggest …

SARAH. I know I've seen that "morphing" thing before …

TYLER. Maybe he drops some change and doesn't see the morphing.

JACK. Some change?

TYLER. Or he needs to put in eye drops.

JACK. Eye drops?

TYLER. He's from England, Jack. He wouldn't be used to the pollen in Transylvania now would he?

SARAH. *Abbott and Costello Meet Frankenstein.* Lon Chaney Jr. turning into the wolfman. It's Gordon's favorite. Tyler, I think you've hit a home run with that.

TYLER. Or I could erase Harker's memory with a gesture and he could play it like he had an aneurysm or a really minor stroke or something. He grabs his skull …

JACK. I don't want to grab my skull.

TYLER. Gordon. What do you think. Really? Your call.

GORDON. That's … That is an incredible idea, Tyler. And, boy, if we had the … time and money to really explore it … It is a great idea … very creative … but …

SARAH. But one of our goals here at the Playhouse is to rehearse slightly beyond the first scene before we open. So the answer is no, Tyler.

GORDON. OK, good. So you're there, Tyler. Jack, you're there. "Vrolak, Ordog, Pokol … " and light's up … "Welcome … "

MARY. I know … like maybe Harker was like a zoology major in college and really fascinated by bats, so …

SARAH. NO! LIGHTS!

TYLER/DRACULA. "Welcome to my house, Mr. Harker. Enter freely and of your own will."

JACK/HARKER. "Count Dracula?"

TYLER/DRACULA. "I am Dracula. And I bid you welcome to my house. Come freely, go safely and leave something of the happiness you bring."

SARAH. Wolf howl.

TYLER. Act with me, Sarah, become the wolf.

SARAH. *(Without affect but plenty of attitude.)* Ow-ow-ow-wooo.

TYLER/DRACULA. "The children of the night. Ah, listen. What music they make." May I stop?

GORDON. Of course. Any time.

TYLER. Good. Thanks. I'm sorry. But there are a lot of issues when you're playing the undead, you know.

GORDON. I know.

TYLER. Where's the house?

GORDON. Behind you? Kind of up-centerish? Does that work for you?

TYLER. So, the door is behind me?

GORDON. It could be below you.

TYLER. Wouldn't it be better if I were in the door? Holding the door? So the first thing we saw was my claw-like fingers slowly wrapping around the door.

MARY. I just got chills!

SARAH. Are you in this scene!? *(Mary sits, meekly.)*

GORDON. Maybe on "Welcome to my house … " as you speak, you could …

TYLER. No, I want to complete it before I speak. I want it to be my significant psychological gesture for the role.

GORDON. But, I think we … need to move … To advance the plot …

SARAH. Gordon? There isn't really a door.

GORDON. Tyler. There isn't really a door.

TYLER. I thought you said it was behind me?

GORDON. The house is behind you.

TYLER. The front door isn't part of the house?

GORDON. *(To Sarah.)* It would be wouldn't it?

SARAH. But it isn't real!

GORDON. But it isn't real!

TYLER. You mean this door isn't real?

GORDON. No. The door isn't real.

TYLER. Well. Perhaps you can tell me how I can justify "Welcome to my house, Mr. Harker … " without a real door?

GORDON. Well, it's an open … environment … space … unit … concept …

TYLER. Maybe someone, anyone, could have told me that in New York *before* I signed the contract! But, here we are. In New

Hampshire. So you just tell me. How do I "welcome-to-my-house-Mr.-Harker" without a door?

SARAH. You could use some of the acting you saved by not morphing?

GORDON. Tyler. There's just … Henry just didn't design a real door for the set.

TYLER. Oh. I see. The set is going to tell me how to act this moment. The stage designer is going to dictate to me, the actor, the one, the only one, who is actually up here …

JACK. … except for me and my eye drops …

TYLER. … actually up here tearing my guts out in front of two hundred people, the designer will tell me how to play this role?

GORDON. We could drape some fabric in the shape of a door … HENRY!

SARAH. Tyler! There is no door! There will not be a door unless you pick one up and "morph" it on with you!

TYLER. I can do that. *(Lights change. The apprentices rearrange the rehearsal set-up from* Dracul, Prince of the Undead *to* Charley's Aunt *during the following exchange.)*

Scene 5

Henry, Gordon, Craig, and Sarah are examining a legal document. Henry carries a hat box.

HENRY. Is this really true?

CRAIG. It's really true.

GORDON. This isn't really true.

SARAH. This is really creepy.

GORDON. We really have to use it?

CRAIG. It's in her will.

SARAH. It's not only really creepy, it's gross.

CRAIG. The lawyer sent it over. Paragraph 7A. "My skull is to be preserved and shall be used to portray the skull of Yorick if and when the Playhouse shall present the play *Hamlet* by William Shakespeare." Paragraph 7B. "The above-stated codicil shall be considered a condition of my bequest of the property to the

Playhouse corporation." Our founder, Ethel Barnes Stein, put it in her will. We're supposed to use her skull for that of Yorick.

SARAH. Creepy, gross and sick. Yuck.

HENRY. I think it's pretty cool.

GORDON. There must be a way out of it.

CRAIG. Not unless we want to give the property back.

GORDON. I guess she really wanted to be in *Hamlet*.

SARAH. Or wanted to make sure no one ever did *Hamlet* at her theatre.

HENRY. You'd better tell Richfield. He's playing the Gravedigger. *(Giving box to Craig.)*

CRAIG. I'm not telling Richfield. He and Daisy are the only ones who actually knew her. You tell him. *(Giving box to Gordon.)*

GORDON. I'm not telling him. It's a technical issue. You tell him, Sarah. *(Giving box to Sarah.)*

SARAH. This is a prop. That's your department, Henry, you take her. *(Giving box to Henry.)*

HENRY. Cool. *(He exits. The rehearsal area has been re-set for the tea scene from Act Two of* Charley's Aunt. *Jack, playing Lord Fancourt Babberly, wears a rehearsal skirt and wig.)*

Scene 6

BRAUN/BRASSET *("Entering" with tea service.)* Tea is served.

TYLER/JACK. Look out, here's tea.

JACK/FANCOURT. Well, what of it? *(Dropping character.)* OK … Now … this is the tea in the hat bit right?

SARAH. Right.

JACK. So … How do we…? Where's Susannah? Where's the director?

SARAH. She said she finds staging rehearsals boring. She wants you guys to just kind of figure it out and then she'll fix it.

JACK. You're kidding me, right?

RICHFIELD. The gag as I recall is really rather simple, but very effective, you'll see. The audience loves this bit. As you know, of course, Lord Fancourt here, "Fanny," puts on the dress and pretends to be "Charley's aunt" so that Charley and Jack can have a chaperone for their dates when Charley's real aunt fails to arrive as scheduled. When the aunt does show up no one knows it's her, so Fanny continues the masquerade by serving tea. Now, Tyler here, playing Jack, holds the cups. Fanny, you pour. At the moment he pulls the cups away from where they're supposed to be, the tea goes in the hat. You keep your attention elsewhere until after you've poured tea in the hat three times. You see it and react. *(Reacts as Fanny.)* Laugh. Jack sees it and reacts. *(Reacts as Jack.)* Laugh. I see it. I react. *(He reacts.)* Enormous laugh. Roars, in fact.

JACK. You do it in rhythm, with the lines?

RICHFIELD. Right. Good instincts.

TYLER. I'll hold out the first two cups after "Do we all take tea?"

JACK. I pour the first two cups for real to set up the gag.

TYLER. I'll hand to Mary.

MARY. I pass to Amy I mean in real life Karma I wish I had your name and then Ian I mean Charley in real stage life like the play *Charley's Aunt.*

JACK. Then the next beat, I keep pouring in rhythm, but the cups aren't there. Tea in hat.

VERNON. And this is supposed to be amusing?

RICHFIELD. That's farce.

VERNON. I hate farce.

JACK. Shall we give it a shot? No books.

RICHFIELD. Flying by the seat of the pants, eh? Run it up and see who salutes. I love stock.

HENRY. *(Passing through.)* This is rep.

RICHFIELD. Rep?

HENRY. Yep.

SARAH. OK. "How do you do I'm Charley's aunt from Brazil where the nuts come from." Oh, look who's here. Susannah.

SUSANNAH. Do you have something to show me yet?

RICHFIELD. I believe we do.

DAISY. Shall we show you the tea beat?

SUSANNAH. By all means. Show me the tea beat.

GORDON. *(Entering, carrying the hat box we have seen previously.)* Has anybody seen Henry? Oh, am I in time to see something here?

SARAH. Yes! Places for the tea beat. And ... "How do you do, I'm Charley's aunt ... "

JACK/FANCOURT. How do you do? I'm Charley's aunt from Brazil where the nuts come from. *(And they play the scene amazingly well: sharp, polished, clean and funny. Far better than they have any right to expect for a first time — but sometimes that happens.)*

DAISY/DONNA LUCIA. How do you do? Do you know I'm most interested in meeting you?

JACK/FANCOURT. Really?

DAISY/DONNA LUCIA. I knew your late husband — intimately!

IAN/CHARLEY. Whatever's the matter, Babs?

JACK/FANCOURT. She knew my late husband, intimately!

TYLER/JACK. *("Entering.")* Well, how are you getting on? Everything's all right, isn't it?

JACK/FANCOURT. No! She knew my late husband intimately!

TYLER/JACK. The deuce!

BRAUN/BRASSET. *("Entering" with tea service.)* Tea is served.

TYLER/JACK. Look out, here's tea.

JACK/FANCOURT. Well, what of it?

TYLER/JACK. You must entertain. Now Donna Lucia will you pour out tea?

JACK/FANCOURT. Oh certainly.

MARY/KITTY. May I help, Donna Lucia?

RICHFIELD/SPETTIGUE. What a cruel interruption! We were getting on so nicely.

JACK/FANCOURT. Do we all take tea? *(Pours two cups of tea. Mary/Kitty delivers. Tyler/Jack holds two cups over the hat for Fanny to fill.)*

DAISY/DONNA LUCIA. You haven't been in England long have you? *(Fanny looks to Jack.)*

TYLER/JACK. Change the subject. *(As he speaks, leaning in to Fanny Babs, he pulls the cups away.)*

JACK/FANCOURT. Change the subject! *(He looks to Donna Lucia and pours into the hat.)*

TYLER/JACK. No. Do you take sugar and cream? *(Jack again places the cups over the hat.)*

JACK/FANCOURT. No. Do you take sugar and cream? *(Fanny Babs looks to Donna Lucia. On "No" Jack pulls the cups away and Fanny Babs pours into hat.)*

TYLER/JACK. Ask her if she takes sugar and cream. *(Cups into position over hat.)*

JACK/FANCOURT. Ask her if she takes sugar and cream. *(Jack pulls away the cups. Fanny pours into the hat.)*

RICHFIELD/SPETTIGUE. I think I should like a little sugar and cream, Donna Lucia. *(Fanny notices hat, then Jack, then Spettigue.)* My hat! My hat!

JACK/FANCOURT. I beg your pardon. *(Fanny pours cream into hat, adds sugar, swirls it around to mix, pours the mixture back into the teapot, hands the hat to Spettigue, taps bottom of it, flipping liquid into Spettigue's eye. Spettigue reacts. During the above, Gordon, Sarah, even Vernon — grudgingly — laugh. They applaud.)*

GORDON. That's wonderful. Terrific. Very. Whoo ... boy ... tight, clean ... That's the gag ...

RICHFIELD. Yes. That's the tea gag isn't it.

GORDON. That's the tea gag. Susannah, well, now it can be said. I was kind of afraid you wouldn't ... you didn't have the ... I mean swimming pools and all that ... But that's the tea gag!

SUSANNAH. I've been thinking about this scene a lot. It is the central event of the play for Lord Fancourt. A man, dressed as a woman. He's pretending to be something and someone he's not and he meets the person he is pretending to be, the real woman. The stakes are as high as they get. The question is ... and no one can answer this but you, Lord Fancourt. Is he/she a transvestite? Or is she/he a cross-dresser? Do you see? The distinction is vital. What do you think?

JACK. I think it's a nineteenth-century farce. I think it's supposed to be funny? Gordon?

GORDON. Yes. A guy in a dress is funny.

SUSANNAH. Unless you're the conflicted soul in the dress.

GORDON. I've worn the dress. I mean I haven't worn a dress not me personally, of course, but I played you know ... Richfield saw my Fanny. Didn't you Richfield?

RICHFIELD. And a fine Fanny it was.

SUSANNAH. Then both of you understand that at heart this is about the anguish of gender. I want to explore that. And I'd like to put in — right at the point in this scene where it all comes to a crisis — a new sound cue, those sinister howling dogs from *Dracula*. That will be your cue to enter with the tea, butler, the howling dogs will be your cue. I think they will begin to suggest the inner torment and rage of gender crisis.

GORDON. But, funny inner torment and rage, right? *(Susannah crosses to Braun. Gordon starts to leave.)*

SARAH. Gordon ...

GORDON. I have to talk to Henry.

SARAH. You're not walking away from this!?

GORDON. Henry! *(He exits.)*

MARY. You know, when you were talking just then about anguish and like inner torment and rage, it kind of reminded me of this scene in *The Epic of Gilgamesh* where I give my body to the gods. I mean the gods kind of looked kind of like anguished and tormented and stuff. Not about their gender identity I guess … 'cause they didn't have any clothes on. Neither did I. So gender identity was real clear.

TYLER. I knew I should have seen that show.

SUSANNAH. OK. Before we get back to "text," I want to explore this scene through physical improvisation.

MARY. Oh wow.

DAISY. Oh, dear.

JACK, VERNON, TYLER, SARAH and RICHFIELD. Oh shit.

SUSANNAH. I mean, what is "Tea" really? Isn't it, at base, a feeding ritual? So, I want to explore this primitive ritual as if you were animals on the African Savannah meeting at dusk at the watering hole. Mary and Karma, you should be … gazelles.

MARY. Oh wow.

KARMA. Way cool.

SUSANNAH. Vernon …

VERNON. If I have to do this — and I'd really rather have a root canal — but if I have to do this I'm going to be the crocodile lying in wait at the water's edge.

SUSANNAH. Excellent. Richfield and Daisy: the aging lion and lioness.

DAISY. Aging?

SUSANNAH. And Jack, Tyler and Ian … a pack of young male orangutangs. You know, of course, the orangutang is innately bisexual, Jack.

JACK. No, I didn't know that.

TYLER. My orangutang is not bisexual. OK? I mean I don't care about your orangutangs, but my orangutang is completely heterosexual. OK? OK?

SUSANNAH. All right now. It's dusk at the water hole …

BRAUN. What am I?

SUSANNAH. What do you think you are?

BRAUN. The butler?

SUSANNAH. A wildebeest. Be a wildebeest.

BRAUN. I don't know how to be a wildebeest.

SUSANNAH. And that is the very reason why we need to improvise this scene.

BRAUN. I'm sorry.

SUSANNAH. And it's dusk at the water hole.

KARMA. Excuse me.

SUSANNAH. Yes?

KARMA. Do you want like gazelle sounds?

SUSANNAH. Of course.

KARMA. What do gazelles sound like?

MARY. They whinny.

KARMA. Whinny? *(Mary whinnies.)* Cool.

SUSANNAH. And the sun sets wearily over the dry, hot, African plain. Two nimble gazelles warily approach the ever-shrinking communal pond … *(The gazelles do so.)* Here we go, now … everybody. *(They all begin to enact their animals with varying degrees of enthusiasm.)* Yes, Lion and Lioness … the proud huntress … and the toothless old alpha male …

RICHFIELD. Toothless…?

SUSANNAH. Stay in it … Keep the imaginative bubble filled … Keep your bubble filled.

RICHFIELD. I think I broke my bubble. I bit it. With my teeth.

DAISY. Richfield.

RICHFIELD. She called me toothless.

SUSANNAH. Orangutangs, you too … Yes. That's it. That's it. And wildebeest, now you … *(To Braun, who has been hanging back, not having a clue as to what is expected.)*

BRAUN. Tea is served! *(Everybody stops.)*

SUSANNAH. No text, wildebeest! No text! Never text!!! Repair the bubble, now. *(She demonstrates how one repairs one's bubble.)* Everybody repair your bubble! … What does it mean, Jack, to be a gender-confused young primate at the communal water hole? Find your center through the breath. Now FILL your bubble with the breath of imagination … FILL your bubble … Now … TEA TIME ON THE SAVANNAH — EXPLORE IT … *(And they do.)* … Yes, yes …

GORDON. *(Entering with Henry and Craig.)* My God! What are they doing?

CRAIG. Is it an orgy?

KARMA. OWW! The alligator bit me!

VERNON. Get too close to the water hole, what the hell do you think's going to happen? And this is Africa for God's sake, I'm not some fat lazy-ass poodle-fed Florida alligator! I'm a crocodile!

JACK. And I'm either a cross-dresser or transvestite I haven't made that choice yet, Susannah, but in any event, who the hell cares, I'm going to law school in seven weeks. *(Stepping out of the rehearsal skirt, one leg in, one leg out.)*

SUSANNAH. Jack, you've given me an idea. Henry! Good, I'm glad you're here. I want to change Lord Fancourt's costume. On the right-hand side it will be a dress. On the left-hand side, trousers. When he faces stage left, we will see the woman. When he faces stage right, we will see the man. When he faces downstage, we will see — and more importantly, understand — the duality. It is an admittedly risky choice but I think, in Jack here, we have an actor …

JACK. … lawyer …

SUSANNAH. … who can pull it off.

SARAH. And in 3-2-1 — yes! Time! End of rehearsal! Thank you, Actors Equity Association. To hell with "one day at a time." Today is the first drink of the rest of your life. *(Lights change. During the following the apprentices set up the rehearsal area for the* Dracul, Prince of the Undead *bedroom scene.)*

Scene 7

CRAIG. *(Entering with several flats of Coca-Cola products.)* Gordon!

GORDON. Yes, Craig.

CRAIG. I have to talk to you.

GORDON. About…?

CRAIG. Pencils. And another matter. But first, pencils. Why does the stage manager insist on putting out an entire number ten can full of pencils on the table in rehearsal? We haven't even opened the first show yet and we have been through three and one half gross of pencils in the stage management area alone.

GORDON. How much is a gross?

CRAIG. One hundred and forty-four.

GORDON. That's … three … four hun …

CRAIG. Five hundred and four.

GORDON. Wow. That's a lot of pencils.

CRAIG. Yes. "Wow." That certainly is "a lot of pencils." But I've got an idea.

GORDON. Good, Craig, I've …

CRAIG. Sarah will assign each actor one and only one pencil. She'll write their name on it at the time the pencil is to be issued. Perhaps on a small piece of tape. Initials would do I suppose. When said pencil has been reduced — by use — to under two and three-eighths inches in length — the size at which for the normal hand it becomes difficult to grip effectively — the actor will return the pencil to stage management and be issued a new pencil.

GORDON. That's a good …

CRAIG. I'm not done. I will recycle these two and three-eighths inch pencils for use in my own office. I have a smallish hand and am willing to forego fresh pencils for the sake of the institution. They also may be used in the scenery shop for marking … boards … for the cutting process … by the saws … thereby eliminating entirely the budgetary need for new pencils in two separate areas of the operation.

GORDON. That's … that's an excellent idea. Got to get to rehearsal …

CRAIG. Gordon! The other matter? We haven't received Mrs. DeMartineau's check yet.

GORDON. I called her months ago.

CRAIG. You have to call her again.

GORDON. Oh no.

CRAIG. Cash flow.

GORDON. Cash flow?

CRAIG. It's not flowing. *(Lights change. Tyler is putting on his cape in the rehearsal area. Mary enters.)*

Scene 8

TYLER. Hey. Good morning! *(With accent, displaying his vampire teeth.)*

MARY. Good morning! Are we rehearsing *Dracula* now? Or is it *Hamlet* or *Charley's Aunt*? I get so confused.

TYLER. *Dracula.*

RICHFIELD. *Dracula*, yes. *(As Van Helsing.)* "So you must be our beautiful Miss Lucy, fiancée of good Mr. Holmwood, daughter to the kindly Mrs. Westenra."

MARY. Nooo … Mina. Fiancée of Mr. Harker. Daughter to the kindly Dr. Seward.

RICHFIELD. Mina! Oh dear. *(He sits aside, studying his script.)*

TYLER. You want to run lines for our scene?

MARY. Which one? I don't have any lines in the only real scene we have together. I just kind of lie there and you talk some about how I'm now "flesh of your flesh ... blood of your blood ... and when your brain says like come to me I'll come to you like for all time ... " and then you suck on my neck.

TYLER. Yeah. Want to rehearse?

MARY. You are so diligent. You always want to rehearse that scene.

TYLER. Well, Mary, that's what being a professional is all about. So. You lie down on the bed ... "And to that end, this ... " *(He "bites" her neck. She giggles uncontrollably.)*

MARY. Tickles...! You know, I've been meaning to ask you something? I mean I think you're really good. The way you can wear those teeth and speak in an accent all at the same time. How come you're not working on like Broadway or something?

VERNON. *(Who has entered in time to overhear Mary's question.)* You want to know why he's not on Broadway? I'll tell you why he's not on Broadway.

TYLER. Vernon ...

VERNON. There are twenty thousand actors in the New York metropolitan area and maybe two hundred are working on Broadway right now and the vast majority of those have vocal cords of titanium alloy genetically engineered to break the glass in a chandelier eight times a week. There's one non-musical currently playing and that is an import from London with six — count 'em, six — American understudies. Now, since it is apparent that without a stroke of luck approaching the supernatural neither Tyler Taylor, nor Vernon Volker for that matter, will be "morphing" into a Broadway actor anytime soon, what's left? Well he can stay in New York and work in one of our prestigious off-Broadway theatres dedicated to the ideals of high art and low pay for — oh — maybe three to four hundred dollars a week. That's if he is lucky and good and has an agent who's sleeping with a casting director who has a brother-in-law who's married to the producer. So? What else is there? If he doesn't mind leaving his wife, his children, his cat ...

TYLER. I'm not married.

VERNON. OK, his bar stool at the West Bank Café — for six, seven, maybe even eight hundred bucks a week he can live out of a suitcase for a couple of months in St. Louis, Cincinnati, Salt Lake, Sioux City, or, God forbid, spend a summer in an un-air-conditioned barn in New Hampshire, like here, for example, at The Playhouse, the Dachau of summer theatres! OR. He can stay in New York, keep his straight job as a waiter, bartender, word processor, or phone sex operator — make triple the money and have a life. But then — we wouldn't be acting, would we? *(Lights change. All exit.)*

Scene 9

It is late at night. Gordon enters, setting the ghost light.

GORDON.
> O that this too, too solid flesh would melt,
> Thaw and resolve itself into a dew.
> Or that the everlasting had not fixed
> His canon 'gainst self slaughter. O God, God,
> How weary, stale, flat and unprofitable seem to me
> All the uses of this world.

How *wear* — y, *stale,* flat, *and,* un-*profit*-able seem ... pro*fit*-able ... *pro*-fit-able ... un-profitable seem to me all the uses of this world.
SARAH. *(Out of the shadows, deep in a corner of the barn.)* Ain't that the truth.
GORDON. Sarah? Is that you?
SARAH. Who did you think? The ghost of Hamlet's father?
GORDON. I just thought I would try to catch a little rehearsal. God knows I need it.
SARAH. I was wondering. You rehearse everybody else and just jump over your parts.
GORDON. Well, I want to get the whole thing on its feet. Besides I shouldn't be playing this part. I'm too old. I look at Jack, who is the right age — or Tyler even — and I just think ...
SARAH. So you're too old. Barrymore played it at your age. Sarah Bernhardt played it at sixty-something. Not only was she too old, she had a wooden leg and she was the wrong sex — oops, excuse me, non-traditionally gendered. Otherly gendered? Whatever, Susannah would have loved it. By the way, we need to discuss that little costume issue that came up the other day.
GORDON. What?
SARAH. What? ... You sounded pretty good just now.
GORDON. No I didn't.
SARAH. OK, you didn't.

38

GORDON. Have you heard about Jack leaving the business? Going to law school in the fall?

SARAH. Yeah?

GORDON. That really pisses me off.

SARAH. Why should it piss you off?

GORDON. I brought him into the company. I hired him.

SARAH. And he's doing the job you hired him for. And doing it well.

GORDON. Of course he's doing it well. It just disturbs me is all.

SARAH. It doesn't piss you off anymore, it disturbs you?

GORDON. Why is that? Why is it that it should disturb me?

SARAH. Because when somebody like Jack leaves the business — somebody with real promise for the big career none of the rest of us ever had or maybe even had the chance to have — when somebody like that leaves, it "disturbs" those of us who remain because it calls into question all the decisions we made along the way or never really made but just let happen. It calls into question our lives. It doesn't have anything to do with Jack. It has to do with us.

GORDON. Oh. You're too smart for your own good. Do you know that?

SARAH. Yes. I do know that. It makes a very good excuse for drinking.

GORDON. Is that...?

SARAH. A little gin and a lot of tonic and ice.

GORDON. Do you think you should?

SARAH. You used to like it when we drank together. We had fun.

GORDON. When we drank together. Then you started drinking by yourself. Even when we were drinking together.

SARAH. *(Overlapping.)* ... even when we were drinking together ...

GORDON. Are you OK?

SARAH. Sure, I'm taking it one drink at a time.

GORDON. How does it feel to be back here?

SARAH. Feels like just another Playhouse summer. Mosquitoes the size of sparrows. Hot and humid enough to make your eyeballs sweat. Actors being actors ... Where did you find Vernon by the way? The Talent Agency for the Terminally Embittered? Henry is being Henry. Craig is being Craig. And Gordon Page is being Gordon Page. You gotta spend some time in *Charley's Aunt* rehearsals, Gordon. We're out of control.

GORDON. I know.

SARAH. Just another Playhouse season. It's good to be home.

Thank you.

GORDON. You're welcome.

SARAH. Do the new ones know?

GORDON. I'm sure Tyler, Richfield and Daisy have filled them in.

SARAH. I'm sure they have. The only thing thicker than the mosquitoes around this place is the gossip. Do the speech again. I promise I won't interrupt. And don't worry about the scansion. Just be simple and quiet — the way you used to be when we were twenty-five and you were burning to play this part and you would read it to me in bed before we turned out the light.

GORDON. "I have of late but wherefore I know not — lost all my mirth ... and indeed, it goes so heavily with my disposition that this goodly frame, the earth, seems to me a sterile promontory; this most excellent canopy the air, look you, this brave o'erhanging firmament, this majestical roof fretted with golden fire — why it appeareth no other thing to me than a foul and pestilent congregation of vapors. What a piece of work is man! How noble in reason! How infinite in faculties! In form and moving how express and admirable In action how like an angel! In apprehension how like a god! ... And yet to me what is this quintessence of dust?" *(He stops. Sarah is crying softly.)* "But break my heart, for I must hold my tongue." *(Lights fade.)*

End of Act One

ACT TWO

Scene 1

GORDON. *(In the barn, on his cell phone.)* Well, Mrs. DeMartineau, I'm not sure I *can* explain that costume, ha ha … Yes. One half did look like a man and the other like a woman. Ha ha … Yes … No … Yes. I mean that is the problem. Wasn't funny. Not funny at all … No. He's a man. All man I should say … No I wouldn't know that. It's not really my job to check that sort of thing … I suppose somehow Susannah, our director, Susannah Huntsmen, your college room-mate's daughter? She directed the play. I didn't. I think she thought it would somehow illuminate the text, make it more relevant … No … Yes … Un-funny is the word … Next? Well, next is *Dracul, Prince of the Undead* … Well I'm afraid that wouldn't be possible, you see we've been rehearsing *Dracul, Prince of the Undead*, we haven't been rehearsing *The Sound of Music* … That's very good, you have a love-ly voice … "Do Re Mi" to you too. Which brings me to the reason for this call, in a way, you see, when we spoke several months ago, you were in Palm Beach, remember? Well, anyway, you had indicat-ed that you were going to send us your annual donation and, well, we haven't gotten it yet and, well, the cash flow … *(Craig enters carrying several flats or large garbage bags of* empty *Coca-Cola product.)*
CRAIG. … is not flowing …
GORDON. … is not flowing Ha ha ha! … No, I don't think I know all the words. In fact I'm sure I don't … I really don't think … Mrs. DeMartineau, I … Really? … OK, "Do, a deer a female deer, Re, a drop of golden sun … "
SARAH. *(Entering.)* What the hell is Gordon doing now?
CRAIG. Speaking with our largest single contributor.
SARAH. Mrs. DeMartineau?
CRAIG. Yes.
SARAH. Does she want her granddaughter to be an apprentice again?
CRAIG. I don't think so. Not after last year.
TYLER. *(Entering.)* Wasn't she one of the Village Girls in *Peer*

41

Gynt, the one who …

SARAH. The one who cried all the time because she thought she was pregnant by the Troll King.

CRAIG. I didn't know that.

SARAH. It was hysterical.

CRAIG. That's why she was upset?

SARAH. Wouldn't you be if you thought you were pregnant by the Troll King?

CRAIG. You thought it was hysterical?

SARAH. Yeah. The pregnancy was hysterical. Imagined.

TYLER. Thank God.

SARAH. What? Tyler…!?

TYLER. Don't look at me. I didn't play the Troll King. I was Peer Gynt.

SARAH. Did you…?

TYLER. What do you mean?

SARAH. Oh no. It was you. It wasn't the Troll King. It was you.

CRAIG. What does she mean, Tyler?

TYLER. Nothing.

GORDON. Got it! She's bringing it round today!

CRAIG. My God, Tyler, what was she, sixteen?

SARAH. Eighteen, maybe.

TYLER. Twenty-two.

SARAH. What, do you check their driver's licenses?

TYLER. Of course.

GORDON. What are you talking about?

SARAH, TYLER and CRAIG. *(Exiting in opposite directions.)* Nothing. *(Henry enters with a long roll of fabric which he proceeds to roll out, measure and mark.)*

GORDON. Henry! How are we? How's the set?

HENRY. Sets. Plural. Set-z. Your little Shakespeare skit and your great big vampire epic. Set-z-z-z. We'll never make it.

GORDON. You always say that and you always pull off a miracle, Henry.

HENRY. Gordon! The special effects in *Dracula* alone …

GORDON. *Dracul, Prince of the Undead.*

HENRY. *Dracoool* … are too much for a theatre with ten times our budget. *(He takes a two and three-eighths inch pencil from behind his ear to mark the fabric.)*

GORDON. I know you can do it …

HENRY. Flying bats, exploding crosses, a sound cue every thirty

42

seconds and God knows how many light cues.

GORDON. *Peer Gynt* had a lot of effects. We flew Peer … sort of … on the flying pig.

HENRY. Yes and Barbara DeMartineau's granddaughter dropped the flying pig and Peer right on the Troll King.

GORDON. That was an accident.

HENRY. The point is, it will be the apprentices running all of these special effects for you all over again. Karma, Ian, and Braun. *(Karma, Ian and Braun enter carrying a straight ladder which they proceed — unsuccessfully — to attempt to maneuver through the barn doors. They turn and reposition the ladder and themselves in every conceivable attitude except the ninety-degree angle to the door at which it would go straight through.)*

GORDON. Great kids.

HENRY. Gordon! These "great" kids have been teching *Dracool* during the day, running *Charley's*-gender-conflicted-*Aunt* in the evening and staying up after the show until six o'clock in the morning to build *Hamlet*. They don't know what play they're doing for God's sake!

GORDON. They'll do fine, Henry. They always do fine. They learn so much from you. You're a real mentor, you know? You give them the confidence to do the amazing things they do do.

HENRY. How appropriately phrased. Hey, guys? Loyal apprenti!? Humble disciples of the craft of Dionysus? TURN THE LADDER SIDEWAYS! *(They do; Karma and Ian exit with the ladder.)*

GORDON. Hey, Brown …

BRAUN. Braun.

GORDON. … what do you know?

BRAUN. *(Exhausted beyond measure.)* I bring the tea on when I hear the howling dogs, that's all I know.

HENRY. I believe my point has been made. *(Sarah enters, singing "Do, a deer … " for Gordon's benefit.)*

GORDON. Sarah? Henry's a bit worried about the effects in *Dracul* …

HENRY. A bit worried?!

GORDON. What do you think? *(Sarah starts to respond, laughs. Starts to respond again, laughs again. Gestures towards, Braun, Ian, and Karma who re-enter and exit, exhausted. Laughs again. Richfield enters, studying his script intently.)*

RICHFIELD. "You must be our beautiful Miss Lucy, fiancée of Mr. Holmwood" … No! Fiancée of Harker … No!!! Beautiful Miss

43

Mina, Mina, Mina, Mina! *(He exits. Sarah laughs uncontrollably.)*

SARAH. *(As if the laughter were a bit much for her bladder.)* Uh-oh, I gotta go. *(She exits.)*

HENRY. I rest my case.

GORDON. You're such a pessimist. *Charley's Aunt* looks great.

HENRY. By the end of the show opening night there was more paint on the actors than there was on the set.

GORDON. The audience loves that sort of thing. Makes them feel part of it. *Live* theatre.

HENRY. Well if they liked *Charley's Aunt*, they are going to love *Dracul, Prince of the Undead*! *(Lights change. Spooky music. The curtain opens for:)*

Scene 2

The Playhouse production of Dracul — Prince of the Undead *by Gordon Page.*

CAST

Van Helsing	*Richfield Hawksley*
Jonathan Harker	*Jack Morris*
Dr. Seward	*Vernon Volker*
Mina Seward	*Mary Pierre*
Dracul, Prince of the Undead	*Tyler Taylor*
Peasant Woman/Bride	*Daisy Coates*
Peasant Woman/Bride	*Susannah Hunstmen*
Peasant Woman/Bride	*Karma Schnieder*
Workman	*Braun Oakes*

Passages in bold indicate technical errors and/or action or dialogue undertaken by the actors in their valiant attempts to keep the sinking ship afloat.

There is a low stone wall upstage, a scrim and moon box behind it, if possible. It is an "open, environment, space, unit, concept." There is a track for a small platform on casters which can be pulled back and forth across the small stage

44

carrying the various furniture pieces. The curtain opens on a low ground fog. Jonathan Harker is surrounded by a group of peasants. They make the two-fingered sign to ward off the "evil eye."

PEASANT WOMAN/DAISY. Ordog ... Pokol ...

PEASANT WOMAN/KARMA. Vrolak ...

HARKER. Please ... What do you want?

PEASANT WOMAN/SUSANNAH. Stregoica ... Vlkoslak ...

PEASANT WOMAN/DAISY. Vrolak ... Ordog ...

HARKER. Does anyone speak English? ... I don't know what you want ... Please ... *(A peasant woman approaches Harker offering him a crucifix.)*

PEASANT WOMAN/KARMA. Vrolak!!! Vrolak!

HARKER. I'm sorry ... I don't understand ... Please.

PEASANT WOMAN/DAISY. Vrolak mean vampire!!! *(Harker and Peasants freeze. Van Helsing enters.)*

VAN HELSING. In the year of our Lord Eighteen Hundred and Ninety-Two a series of documents came into my hands. These diaries, newspaper articles and letters of dear friends one to another have here been placed in an order to reveal a story so totally at variance with the possibilities of contemporary belief as to appear the ravings of madmen. We offer no proofs. You have only my word before God that what follows is pure and simple fact.

PEASANTS. Ordog ... Pokol ... Stregoica ... Vrolak ... Vlkoslak ...
(The peasants exit. Lights change. Music. A wolf howls. A man clad in black appears. He carries a door. Harker turns to look. A "claw-like" hand appears around the door. Harker drops some change and subsequently puts in eye drops as Dracula "morphs" from wolf to human form.)

DRACULA. Welcome to my house, Mr. Harker. Enter freely and of your own will.

HARKER. Count Dracula?

DRACULA. I am Dracula. And I bid you welcome to my house. Come in. The night air is chill and you must need to eat and rest. *(Lights change. They cross through the door. A small table and two chairs glide on.)* You will, I trust, excuse me that I do not join you; but I never eat ... food.

HARKER. Thank you, Count. My employer, Mr. Hawkins, extends his regrets that he could not come personally, but he suffers from gout.

DRACULA. I am confident you will serve my needs, Harker, Jonathan. But come, tell me of England and of the house you have purchased for me. *(A wolf howls in the distance.)* Ah, listen, the children of the night *(Sound of a tape rewinding.)* what music they make.

HARKER. Why do you wish to go to London, Count?

DRACULA. It shall make me feel young again. *(Dracula laughs, the laugh building to a wild frenzy. He makes a gesture. Harker holds his skull. Lights change. Dracula exits — with the door.)*

HARKER. God help me! "What has old Mr. Hawkins, my employer, suffering from gout and unable to make this journey got me into now," I ask myself. At once I began to search the castle. I ran up the stairs to the highest tower. As I leaned from the window, the wild crags of the Carpathians arrayed before me in the bloodless light of a full moon … *(Behind the scrim, silhouetted by the moon, arms and cape extended, is Dracula. He swings the cape in to cover his face, morphing into a bat. Lights blackout behind the scrim. A bat flies across the stage on a wire.)* What manner of man is this! God preserve me! … May 30, 1892, in the awful light of a gray dawn, I vainly watch as a band of Transylvanian peasants load fifty great wooden boxes on their crude wheeled handcarts and draw them slowly through the castle gates. The Count intends to travel to London and I am to be left … HERE! Left to them! The horrible brides of Dracula! *(Lights up behind the scrim on the horrible Brides of Dracul, Prince of the Undead.)* I must attempt to scale the castle wall! God be merciful. *(Jonathan exits.)*

SEWARD. *(Entering with a newspaper. **But the lights are up on the opposite side of the stage.**)* The Whitby Daily Telegraph, Eight August, 1892. *(**Lights suddenly switch to Seward.**)* "One of the strangest and most sudden storms on record has just been experienced here. It was centered upon a foreign vessel that had strangely appeared in the harbor." *(**Lights suddenly out on Seward and up on the opposite side of the stage. Seward moves towards the light, at which point, of course, the light goes out and comes back up where it was supposed to be in the first place.**)* "There was not a living soul aboard, only the body of one poor seaman whose throat had been strangely torn open as if by some animal. And strangely, a large and wolflike dog was seen leaping from the vessel. The strange schooner has only a small cargo — a number of strange large wooden boxes filled with earth." Hmmm. Strange.

MINA. *(Mina's bed tracks on. Mina is writing in her diary.)* Eleven

August. Jonathan, my fiancé, has returned from Transylvania, but so changed. He will not speak of the events that occurred. My, my the fog is thick tonight. *(A sudden blast of fog.)* I am so tired … so, so, tired … *(Music. The distant howl of a wolf.)*

DRACULA. *(Voice-over.)* Come … Come … *(Mina wanders through the fog.)* Come to me my love … I am eternity … I am the life … I am the blood. Come … Come … Come … The blood is the life. *(Mina crosses downstage. Dracula appears out of the fog. **Another big blast of fog.** He envelopes her in his cape — **she giggles uncontrollably then stops suddenly as he reveals her.** He exits. She crosses back to the bed.)*

SEWARD. My daughter, Mina, has been extremely tired and weak lately.

TYLER. *(Voice-over.)* **Sarah, what the hell is going on with the fog?**

SARAH. *(Voice-over.)* **Turn off your mike!**

TYLER. *(Voice-over.)* **Shit!**

SEWARD. **Yes, shhhh … it is strange, these voices in the night …** I have written to my old friend and professor Abraham Van Helsing. He is not only a medical doctor, but philosopher, meta-physician and expert on strange diseases … *(Van Helsing enters with Harker. Seward crosses into the scene.)*

VAN HELSING. *(Confidently.)* So you must be our beautiful **Miss Lucy,** fiancée of good **Mr. Holmwood,** daughter to the kindly **Mrs. Westenra.**

MARY. **Nooo … I'm. Mina. Fiancée of Mr. Harker. Daughter to the kindly Dr. Seward.**

VAN HELSING. **Of course you are! Whatever your name,** I have the so great pleasure to meet you because you are so beloved. They tell me you are a trifle pale.

MINA. I am fine, Doctor Van Helsing … absolutely fine.

VAN HELSING. Ah … So … Now, Miss … *(Carefully.)* Mina, forgive me. I wish to feel the glands in your throat. *Gott in Himmel!*

SEWARD. What is it?

HARKER. Doctor? Is there anything wrong.

VAN HELSING. Nothing. Nothing, my young friends … Miss **Lu-Mina,** you have two small puncture wounds on your throat here. Do you know where you got them?

MINA. No. No. I don't know! Leave me alone!

VAN HELSING. Oh, Miss **Lucy.**

HARKER. Oh, **Miss Mina.** Oh my God. **Mina.**

47

MINA. Jonathan. Hold me. Don't go away. Hold me.

VAN HELSING. We will step into the next room, *ja? (Van Helsing and Seward cross away. Jonathan follows. The bed disappears. A small settee is pushed on by means of a rather obvious stick.)* Just as I expected. There can be no doubt.

HARKER. No doubt as to what, Professor?

VAN HELSING. Have you never heard of … THE VAMPIRE!

HARKER. THE VAMPIRE! In England?

SEWARD. THE VAMPIRE! In the nineteenth century?

VAN HELSING. Yes! The Vampire! In England! In the nineteenth century! I have here a letter from my good friend Professor Szgany of Budapest. This letter will tell us everything we need to know about this vampire. I have the letter here … **no, it must be here … ah! … no … I seem to have forgotten the letter from my friend Professor Szgany of Budapest …**

SEWARD. **… Perhaps … you can remember its content …**

VAN HELSING. **Huh?**

HARKER. **Yes, maybe you can remember what it said.**

VAN HELSING. **No. I don't think I can remember my friend Professor Szgany's letter.**

SEWARD. **Well, Professor … do you suppose, this vampire could possibly be the great Vlad Dracul of Transylvania, the prince who won his name by fighting with the Turks?**

VAN HELSING. **Correct. He fought Turks in the fifteenth century. He is also called Vlad Tepes *(Pronounced "Tsepesh," which of course causes Richfield to spit profusely in Vernon's face.)* which translate to … which translate to … *(Sotto voce.)* Help! Help!**

HARKER. **I know. It translates to "Vlad The Impaler." … I studied Transylvanian at Cambridge.**

SEWARD. **Now why would he be called the "Impaler," Professor?**

HARKER. **Yes, what do you know about that, Professor?**

VAN HELSING. **Nothing. But if I had my letter … *(Richfield tries to leave the stage.)***

SEWARD. *(Seward stops him.)* **No, Doctor, please don't leave us now! Do you suppose he can appear in different forms? Perhaps, the rat, the wolf and the bat …**

HARKER. **I suppose he could! Hmmm … Interesting.**

SEWARD. **Yes … and strange.**

VAN HELSING. **Yes. Interesting and strange. *(Richfield again*** *tries to leave the stage. They prevent him from doing so.)*

SEWARD. **How do you suppose he manages to stay alive ... I mean, to live, for all those centuries?** *(He taps two fingers on his neck and makes a sucking sound.)*

HARKER. **Yes, Professor, how does he stay alive century, after century, after long, long century ...** *(He pretends to cut his finger and suck the blood.)*

VAN HELSING. **AH! I know!** He flourishes by replenishing his own life with the blood life of the living!

HARKER. The blood life of the living! Surely, Van Helsing, you can't mean there are vampires in this day and age?

VAN HELSING. He is called Nosferatu — the undead — and your mortal weapons are powerless against him!

SEWARD. Good Lord! If this is true how are we to begin? Even if we find him how can we possibly destroy him?

VAN HELSING. **I don't know ... I have forgotten the letter.**

SEWARD. **Well, perhaps, Doctor, you should have memorized the goddamn letter.**

VAN HELSING. **Memorized?**

SEWARD. **Yeah. In rehearsal.**

HARKER. **Yes, I'm sure what Dr. Seward means is that in preparation for our little meeting today, in "rehearsal" as it were, for our meeting here in nineteenth-century London, you might have committed it to memory.**

MINA. *(Entering, to save the day.)* **I have it! I've found the letter, Professor, from your old friend Professor Szgany in Budapest.**

VAN HELSING. **Oh, thanks ...**

HARKER. **Yes. Thank you, Mina, darling.**

VAN HELSING. *(Reading.)* Yes. He can be destroyed, but only by one method. A wooden stake must be driven through the vampire's heart.

HARKER. Surely, Van Helsing, you can't mean **... Mina, back to bed now, darling.**

MINA. **No, but, I'm on in ...**

HARKER. **You see, now that we have the letter.** *(He propels her offstage. A frantic clumping backstage. If possible we see Mina's head silhouetted against the moon or a backdrop as she tries to make her crossover. A pause until the clumping stops.)*

SEWARD. A stake through the heart!

HARKER. From that tower, I watched all those boxes carted out through the gate, and I knew ...

SEWARD. Of course, the boxes! *(Mina enters.)*

MINA. I heard your voices, so I thought I'd …

HARKER. Mina darling, It's so good to see you up and about, why, you haven't been out of bed for a week.

SEWARD. Jonathan, what was the name of the estate you transferred to Count Dracula?

HARKER. Carfax! Carfax was the name!

SEWARD. Carfax Abbey! Good God man, do you know what you are saying?

MINA. Isn't Carfax the estate…? *(Pointing stage left.)*

SEWARD. Yes. No more than a mile across the heath. *(Pointing stage right.)*

HARKER. Then we've got him! *(The settee is pulled offstage.)* Our little search party set forth … We crossed the heath, then kept to the shadow of the wall as we approached the house. *(Sound of a door creaking open and shut — but not in sync with the mimed action.)*

HARKER. Look for a flight of stairs leading down to the cellar.

SEWARD. My God! What's that? *(A bat flies across the stage.)*

HARKER. It's a bat!

SEWARD. Shoot it! *(Harker shoots. The gun does not fire.)*

VAN HELSING. You cannot kill that bat with your little gun!

HARKER. **I didn't.**

SEWARD. **The gun didn't fire.**

VAN HELSING. **Ah hah, you see …**

SEWARD. Doctor! The stairs! Right over here. *(Harker and Van Helsing follow him offstage.)*

MINA. *(Entering elsewhere.)* I can't quite recall how I fell asleep last night. I remember hearing a distant gunshot **… or perhaps it was only a distant click, click.** *(The gun now fires from offstage.)* and I remember the sudden barking of dogs **… yes … I do remember the sudden barking of dogs … barking dogs** *(No dog bark. A moment as Mary "repairs her bubble.")* … And then there was a silence over everything, silence so profound that I got up and looked out the window. All was dark and silent, *(Now the dogs bark.)* not a thing seemed to be stirring, not a sound … *(And they bark again.)* … but all to be grim and fixed as silent death. *(And again they bark.)*

DRACULA. *(Entering.)* I bring you life … eternal life … The blood is the life … the blood is the life …

BRAUN. *(Entering as "Brasset," the Butler in* Charley's Aunt.*)* **Tea is served.**

MINA. ... **Ah, here's tea.**

DRACULA. **Tea?**

MINA. **Yes ... You must serve.**

DRACULA. **Yes ... The tea is the life ... the tea is the life ...** *(Sotto voce, attempting to disguise the words.)* **Wrong play.**

BRAUN. **But I heard the barking dogs!**

MINA. **Do you take sugar and cream?**

DRACULA. *(Sotto voce.)* **Wrong wrong play ...**

MINA. **I've been waiting so long to meet you, you must be Charley's aunt from Brazil ...**

DRACULA. **I have lived in many centuries, many continents. Yes, even in Brazil I am known as the Impaler.** *(Sotto voce.)* **Wrongplaywrongplaywrongplay! Go back! Go back!** *(He attempts to hypnotize Braun.)* **Go back ... to where the nuts come from so she can be mine for all eternity. I morph you away ... away ... away ...** *(Braun exits. Dracula picks up Mina. As he is about to bite her neck, she places the tea cup to his lips. He carries her off.)*

HARKER. *(Entering, followed by Seward and Van Helsing.)* Damn! There are no more boxes here.

SEWARD. Thirty-three boxes. Seventeen missing!

VAN HELSING. How are we going to find them?

HARKER. All fifty boxes were shipped directly to Carfax. Some freight company carted seventeen away. And somewhere, there is a workman who remembers.

VAN HELSING. Excellent thinking, Arthur!

SEWARD/HARKER. **Jonathan!**

HARKER. Eight October. I have made a list of every freight company in greater London. We have split it in two. I am off to tackle the first half, Dr. Seward the second. *(Lights up elsewhere on Seward and a Workman, played by Braun in a false beard.)*

WORKMAN. Yes, Dr. Seward, here it is. Our men delivered "five boxes of common earth" to Jamaica Lane, Bermondsley. *(Blurting it out.)* **I'm sorry about the tea.**

SEWARD. **Yes, boxes of earth, not interested in boxes of tea.** "Jamaica Lane." Thank you, my good man. *(Seward and the Workman exit.)*

HARKER. *(Entering.)* Mina, Mina ... We've got him! *(Mina's bed glides on stage, **but well beyond its planned position.**)*

MINA. Got him? What do you mean. *(**The bed moves back a few feet.**)*

HARKER. Your father has located the boxes. *(The bed moves forward a few feet.)*

MINA. Oh Jonathan, thank God! At last perhaps this awful nightmare is over.

HARKER. Perhaps you're right, darling ... **darling? ... darling!!!** *(The bed is pulled rapidly and mistakenly offstage. There is a crash. The bed smoothly glides back into position. A small broken flat hangs off a bed post. Mina holds a bent and twisted lighting instrument in her lap.)*

MINA. Oh Jonathan, thank God! At last perhaps this awful nightmare is over. *(She hands the light to Jonathan.)*

HARKER. **I don't think so.** Darling ... *(Mina shivers.)* What is it, darling?

MINA. I don't know, darling. I don't know. Oh, please just hold me! *(As Harker holds her we hear faint and disturbing music. The stage covers with fog. A wolf howls. Harker and Mina respond. They are both now in a trance.)*

DRACULA. *(Voice-over.)* Rise, Jonathan Harker ... you are mine ... My thoughts are your thoughts ... *(Harker crosses slowly away from the bed. Dracula enters. He carries the door. He crosses through the door, closes it. But his cape is caught. He attempts to open the door. The handle comes off in his hand. He tosses it offstage.)* **Braun! The cape! ... I mean, brawny minions of the undead ... release the cape ... release the cape, lords of the underworld ... Let go of the goddamn cape!** *(He picks up the door and crosses to the bed.)*

MINA. Jonathan.

DRACULA. Silence. A sound and I shall dash his brains out before your eyes ... *(A gesture from Dracula. Jonathan grabs his skull and falls to his knees.)* You are now to me flesh of my flesh, blood of my blood, kin of my kin. Now and forever you shall come to my call. When my brain says "come" to you, you shall cross land or sea to do my bidding; and to that end this! *(Dracula attempts to bite her neck, **but the cape prevents him from doing so. He bites her arm. Mina giggles uncontrollably.** The lights go to black. He exits with the door:)* **Ah, shit.** *(Lights come up. Mina is collapsed across the bed, Harker on the floor.)*

VAN HELSING. Oh my God! **Lucy! Arthur!**

SEWARD. Oh my God! **Mina! Jonathan!** Quickly, Doctor. You see to Mina. *(He races to Jonathan, Van Helsing to Mina.)* He's been drugged ... or in some sort of trance. Jonathan! Jonathan! *(He slaps Jonathan to wake him. **Jonathan does the "knap" out of rhythm.)***

52

Is she alive?

MINA. Jonathan …

HARKER. Oh, thank God … thank God you're alive.

VAN HELSING. My friends, we must this day hunt out this vampire's lair — sterilize his remaining earth boxes — and drive this monster to bay! *(The bed moves offstage.)*

SEWARD. We quickly made our way to Jamaica Lane where we discovered more of the great boxes filled with soil from the vampire's native Transylvania.

HARKER. There's only sixteen boxes here.

SEWARD. Thirty-three at Carfax …

VAN HELSING. And now only sixteen here. That makes **forty-eight.**

HARKER. **Nine. Forty-nine!**

VAN HELSING. **Ach yes, Einstein, forty-nine!**

HARKER. My God! Mina … I must get back to Mina.

VAN HELSING. No. Wait. Shhhh. Now he comes. To your places. *(They hide. The lights dim. A bat flies across the stage. Dracula enters as if "morphing" from bat to human form. Van Helsing steps out, holding a crucifix.)*

DRACULA. Van Helsing! *(He hisses and backs away. Harker and Seward step out blocking his path.)*

VAN HELSING. So we finally meet, Count Dracula. I have awaited this moment.

DRACULA. I too, Van Helsing, the great Van Helsing! *(With a gesture he places Harker and Seward in a trance.)* They are weak. You are stronger. But you will serve me, all the same. Come to me. Come … You shall obey. *(Van Helsing weakens. He staggers a step forward.)* Yesss … *(Van Helsing drops the crucifix to his side.)* You are mine …

VAN HELSING. AHHH! *(With an enormous effort Van Helsing raises the crucifix into the vampire's face. Dracula snarls, grabbing the cross, which bursts into flames. **But it doesn't.**)*

VAN HELSING. You see the holy cross bursts into flames at your unholy touch!

DRACULA. **No it doesn't.**

VAN HELSING. **Yes, it does.**

HARKER. **Yes, I think I saw it burst into flames at his unholy touch.**

DRACULA. **No it didn't.** *(Now it does. SEE NOTES.)* Oww! *(Snarling with inarticulate rage, Dracula pulls back.)* You know

53

nothing. You fools! Pitiful fools! You think you have left me without a place to rest, but I have one last box … Search as you will, you shall never find me for my revenge has just begun. I shall **th**leep in my earth-box**th** for **th**enturies. *(He re-adjusts his teeth, which have slipped, causing him to lisp.)* Hear my prophecy! *(He exits strongly — straight into the proscenium or the edge of a flat.)* Oww. *(A bat flies out from where he has disappeared.)*

HARKER. Look!

SEWARD. He has escaped us! *(But the bat snags halfway across the stage.)*

HARKER. No! He hasn't escaped us. He remains … where he is!

SEWARD. *(The bat backs up a few feet, bounces for a moment, then advances center where it flaps helplessly.)* But look! Now he escapes us … not.

HARKER. Wait! I think he is disappearing, becoming invisible. I can't see him anymore. Can you see him, Dr. Seward.

SEWARD. No. I can see him no longer. Can you see him Dr. Van Helsing.

VAN HELSING. Yes.

HARKER. No. I don't think you can. A mist is growing before our eyes. *(The lines supporting the bat go slack and the bat slowly sinks to the floor where it continues to flap. The actors stare at it helplessly. Finally …)*

VAN HELSING. *(Front.)* If you believe in vampires, clap your hands … yes, clap your hands as hard as you can and maybe …

SEWARD. *(Stopping him.)* Professor, NO!

HARKER. No, Doctor Van Helsing! I think this night has been too much for him.

SEWARD. I'll take care of this bat. *(He picks up the bat and with it, of course, the lines. Someone pulls from offstage. A brief tug of war. Vernon gives a mighty pull and Sarah falls on stage holding the other end. A tug on the line from the other side. Vernon pulls back, hard. Gordon falls on stage. Sarah "morphs" into a "bat," picks up the puppet bat, "flies" offstage. Gordon, getting the idea, "morphs" into a wolf and exits.)* Look! There it goes.

HARKER. Yes, look, there they both go! The evil one has morphed himself in twain …

SEWARD. He has escaped us!

HARKER. Oh God! All is lost. Mina is lost.

VAN HELSING. No, Jonathan. Of this I am sure. There is but one more earth box and we shall find it if we have to track him all the way back to Transylvania! And so we shall!!!

HARKER. And so we did!

VAN HELSING. Now, we enter the castle.

HARKER. For hours we searched every inch of the castle, forcing doors, ripping away curtains and shutters. I am appalled by my horrid memories of the place.

SEWARD. I found it! The earth box. The last one. *(Seward pushes on the earth box.)*

VAN HELSING. Now. Quickly, there is little time. The sun is setting. *(Seward pries at the lid of the box with a crowbar.)* Jonathan, the mallet and stake! *(Harker races to get them. The Brides enter.)*

HARKER. Oh my God! There they are, the horrid brides of Dracul, Prince of the Undead!!!

BRIDES. No! No! Leave the master, leave the master alone! *(Seward and Harker drive the Brides offstage with their crucifixes.)*

BRIDE/DAISY. I'm melting …

VAN HELSING. Now! Harker. For God's sake hurry. The sun!

SEWARD. It's almost gone. The sun is almost gone! *(Seward pulls off the lid of the box, revealing the sleeping Dracula. Suddenly, his arm shoots out, taking Seward by the throat.)*

VAN HELSING. Harker! The mallet and stake.

HARKER. **I can't find the mallet and stake. I thought you were supposed to bring the mallet and stake.**

VAN HELSING. **There must be a mallet and stake somewhere backstage … I mean around the backstage of this castle … in the wing of the castle.**

HARKER. **Which wing…?**

VAN HELSING. **The stage left wing … of the castle.** *(Harker exits.)*

SEWARD. *(Gasping.)* **Do something! Damn it, do something!**

VAN HELSING. **I'll hit him with the crowbar!**

DRACULA and SEWARD. **NO!**

DRACULA. **Shit man, not a crowbar! … You cannot kill me with your crowbar … Your puny bar of crow!**

HARKER. *(Entering left.)* **One of the brides took the mallet and stake to the stage right … wing of the … castle. I think she's been converted to the good side of the force. Yes. She has! Here she comes.** *(Karma enters with the mallet and stake.)* **May the force be with you, sister. Here.** *(Handing the stake to Van Helsing.)*

VAN HELSING. Now Arthur …

JONATHAN. **Jonathan!**

VAN HELSING. Now, now, now! *(Van Helsing holds the stake over Dracula's heart. Jonathan slams the mallet down.* **He misses and hits Van Helsing's fingers.)** **OWWW!**

JONATHAN. **Sorry.**

VAN HELSING. **Do it yourself.** *(Jonathan hits the stake. A horrific shriek from Dracula. He releases Seward, who staggers off. Harker strikes the second blow and third blow. Mina enters.)*

HARKER. Look, look … Mina! … God is merciful …

MINA. Is he dead. *(**The stake drops from Dracula's armpit; he replaces it quickly and recovers, as if dead.**)* Thank God! Oh, Jonathan, at last our awful nightmare is over. *(They exit.)*

VAN HELSING. Yes **Lucy …**

CAST. *(From offstage.)* **MINA!!!**

VAN HELSING. … at last our awful nightmare is over. *(**Music, at the wrong speed. Lights fade to black, but not completely. Curtain closes … sort of.**)*

Scene 3

The barn is dark. Gordon sits by himself, unseen. Sounds of a party float in from outside.

HENRY. *(Entering, followed by Craig.)* That's two weeks in a row!

CRAIG. I wouldn't ask if we didn't really need it.

HENRY. I'll bet Macy's never misses their payroll!

CRAIG. Gordon's already agreed.

HENRY. Do you have any idea when we might get paid?

CRAIG. I don't know. And after tonight I wouldn't bet *Dracul, Prince of the Undead* is going to bail us out. But at least this will give me enough cash to pay the actors so Equity won't shut us down.

HENRY. Sixty…?

CRAIG. Sixty-seven.

HENRY. Sixty-seven years. Jeez. *(They exit. Gordon rises. Sarah enters.)*

SARAH. It could have been worse.

GORDON. Could it?

SARAH. No one died. I thought that was pretty funny when Richfield went for Tyler with the crowbar.

GORDON. Yeah. Pretty funny.

SARAH. Don't worry about it, Gordon. It's only one performance. We'll sort out the technical stuff. Next time the actors will remember their props. Richfield might even remember some of the right names.

GORDON. Yeah.

SARAH. I thought I morphed my way out of that scene pretty well, don't you? No? That was supposed to be funny. I'm going to the party. You coming?

GORDON. In a minute. OK?

SARAH. It's only a play, Gordon.

GORDON. Yeah. It's only a play. Only a company of actors, like Daisy and Richfield, who have been coming here since they were teenagers. And Craig — who has no other life. It's their home. Andy McAllister was out here tonight. He saw his first play at this theatre in 1938 and tonight he brought his grandson to see his first play. It's only a sixty-seven-year-old theatre.

SARAH. I'm sorry, honey. *(She exits. A brief moment. Vernon and Jack cross through on their way to the party. They do not see Gordon in the shadows.)*

VERNON. It's pathetic. That's the only word for it. Not just the tech stuff. The script. The direction. Everything. It's pathetic. He's pathetic.

JACK. Gordon?

VERNON. Who else? Our "Autistic Director." The man's the laughing stock of the American theatre. Can't wait for *Hamlet* …

JACK. Vernon, shh … *(They exit.)*

GORDON.

    O that this too, too solid flesh would melt,

    Thaw and resolve itself into a dew.

    Or that the everlasting had not fixed

    His canon 'gainst self-slaughter. O God, God,

    How weary, stale, flat and unprofitable

    Seem to me all the uses of this world!

(During the above, Gordon rises, makes some slight alteration in dress — it is a modern-dress Hamlet — and disappears behind the curtain. The speech continues as a voice-over. The company enter, setting chairs, a costume rack and a props table. The curtain opens, revealing the rear side of muslin-covered flats and we transition into the performance of Hamlet, *which we will view from the backstage perspective.)*

GORDON/HAMLET. "It is not, nor it cannot come to good. But break my heart for I must hold my tongue."

HORATIO/JACK. *(Entering with Susannah and Ian as Marcellus and Bernardo.)* "Hail to your Lordship!"

DAISY. How do you think it's going?

RICHFIELD. Not bad. Not so bad at all.

DAISY. Good. I forgot to tell you. Kisses on your opening, old friend! You too, Vernon.

VERNON. Kisses on my opening!?

TYLER. *(To Braun, who is searching the prop table.)* Have you seen Mary? *(Braun shakes his head.)*

RICHFIELD. You know, you've been saying that for years, Daisy, "kisses on your opening" and perhaps you might think about just saying "break a leg" or something.

DAISY. Why?

RICHFIELD. Well, I mean, "kisses on your opening"...?

DAISY. What?

RICHFIELD. I mean it suggests ... kisses on your "opening."

DAISY. Yes. Exactly. Kisses on your opening night. Are you the Ghost now?

RICHFIELD. Nope. Ghost first, Polonius now, ghost again, then the Gravedigger and finally the English Ambassador. Quite the workout.

TYLER. Where's Mary?

RICHFIELD. Haven't seen her.

JACK/HORATIO. "My duty to your honor." *(Exiting from* Hamlet *with Susannah/Marcellus and Ian/Bernado to "backstage.")*

TYLER. Is it OK out there?

RICHFIELD. Yes. I think it's OK.

TYLER. *(Mary enters.)* Mary, where have you been? You almost made us late. Here I am, standing here, trying to prepare ... Emotional preparation is really the key to acting ... isn't that right, Jack?

JACK. I don't know anything about acting anymore. I'm a law student. Ask me about torts.

GORDON. *(Overlapping.)* "Foul deeds will rise, / though all the earth o'erwhelm them to men's eyes." *(He "exits" to "backstage." Mary "enters" on her cue.)* Tyler!? "Foul deeds will rise?"

TYLER/LAERTES. Shit! *("Entering.")* "My necessaries are embarked./ Farewell. And sister as the winds give benefit … "

GORDON. What happened with Tyler?

RICHFIELD. Mary was a bit … well actually, Tyler was a bit … You know, it seems kind of OK out there.

GORDON. Yes, it does seem kind of OK out there.

RICHFIELD/POLONIUS. *("Entering.")* "Yet here, Laertes? Aboard, aboard for shame … "

GORDON. *(Sitting next to Daisy.)* They're listening. They seem to be right with it.

DAISY. Well it's not too hot. They don't listen when they're too hot or when it's too humid. The temperature-humidity index is really the key to audience listening.

GORDON. We've got the barn doors open and there's a nice breeze coming through the screens.

DAISY. And the mosquitoes. They won't listen if they're waving their programs at the mosquitoes.

GORDON. Not too many mosquitoes for some reason.

DAISY. They respond to the temperature-humidity index too.

GORDON. They really do seem to be listening. *(Tyler "exits" to backstage.)*

DAISY. The mosquitoes? I'm so glad. Kisses on your opening, dear.

HENRY. *(Entering with Braun.)* What do you mean you can't find it?

BRAUN. I can't find it.

HENRY. Did you set it on the prop table and check it against your list?

BRAUN. I set it on the prop table and checked it against my list.

HENRY. You lost the skull of Yorick?

BRAUN. Oh God.

HENRY. You lost the skull of Ethel Barnes Stein?

BRAUN. Oh God, oh God.

HENRY. Well, you damn well better find it or it will be your skull we'll be using for a prop!

BRAUN. Oh God, oh God, oh God!

MARY/OPHELIA. *(Mary/Ophelia and Richfield/Polonius "exit.")* "I shall obey my Lord."

GORDON/HAMLET. *(Gordon/Hamlet and Jack/Horatio "enter.")* "The air bites shrewdly. It is very cold … "

59

TYLER. Thanks a lot, Mary, you made me late.

MARY. Just because I won't sleep with you, you blame me for you messing up our entrance?

TYLER. No ... Not just because ... *(Mary exits to the dressing room. Tyler notices the entire company looking at him. They look away.)* No ... Not.

GORDON/HAMLET. " ... it is a custom more honored in the breach than in the observance ... " *(We hear a gentle laugh of recognition from the audience.)*

RICHFIELD. Got a nice laugh there ... Not bad.

VERNON. Amazing.

RICHFIELD. Amazing?

VERNON. Gordon Page? "Hamlet"? Amazing.

RICHFIELD. Perhaps if you weren't upstaging him at every opportunity ...

VERNON. I am not upstaging him.

TYLER. You play the last scene against the back wall, man.

VERNON. I do not! ... Gordon Page as "Hamlet." And even I have to admit he's going to be OK.

TYLER. Maybe better than OK.

DAISY. Yes. Better than OK. Because the only thing he's trying to do out there is to tell a story simply and honestly. And that's all they really want, you know. To sit in the dark and listen to stories. And the best we can ever do is just that. Tell them a good story.

TYLER. And this is a good story.

DAISY. And the other thing they want is a nice temperature-humidity index.

VERNON. He has no damn business doing Hamlet even if I am upstaging him.

JACK/HORATIO. "Look my Lord, it comes!"

GORDON/HAMLET. "Angels and ministers of grace defend us!" *(The Ghost/Richfield enters. Lights and sound indicate a passage of time from* Hamlet *Act One, Scene 4 to Act Three, Scene 2. During this and subsequent transitions we might hear a sound collage of famous lines from the appropriate section of* Hamlet *and a flat might be back-lit so the actors' movement is silhouetted. The company rearrange themselves backstage. Gordon/Hamlet and The Players [Susannah as the Player King, Karma, the Player Queen and Ian as Lucianus] are "on stage." During the following Braun crosses through looking for the skull. Mary quietly rehearses an upcoming speech. Tyler walks through his duel. Daisy and Richfield are in quiet conversation. Jack studies his*

Introduction to Torts. *But by the end of the following speech, which we hear more and more clearly over the monitors, the company slowly begins to pay real attention, until by the end — all are completely still and rapt. Voice-over:)* "Speak the speech, I pray you, as I pronounced it to you, trippingly on the tongue … Nor do not saw the air too much with your hand, thus, but use all gently … Suit the action to the word, the word to the action; with this special observance, that you o'erstep not the modesty of nature: for anything so overdone is from the purpose of playing, whose end, both at the first and now, was and is, to hold as t'were the mirror up to nature; to show virtue her own feature, scorn her own image, and the very age and body of the time his form and pressure … Go make you ready … What ho, Horatio!"

JACK/HORATIO. *("Entering.")* "Here sweet Lord, at your service." *(Lights and sound indicate a passage of time from Act Three, Scene 2 to Act Four, Scene 4. Henry and Braun enter from opposite sides, both still searching.)*

HENRY. No?

BRAUN. No.

HENRY. Well then, maybe you'd better give Gordon a little re-write. Something along the lines of: "Alas, poor Yorick, I knew him Horatio, before he lost his head!" *(Henry exits.)*

BRAUN. *(In desperation.)* Does anyone know where the head is?

VERNON. Out the door and to your right. *(Braun exits.)*

TYLER. *(Sitting next to Mary. She moves a seat away.)* So you're still mad at me.

MARY. I'm not mad. I made my entrance on time.

TYLER. Well, you cut it so damn close that it broke my concentration. Preparation and concentration and listening are …

MARY. You know, I could have maybe fallen in love with you for real except you're always trying to do some bullshit actor-guy thing on me!

TYLER. "Bullshit actor-guy thing"!? Oh that's really smart, some "bullshit actor-guy thing." … Did you just say…?

MARY. I've got to go "prepare."

GORDON/HAMLET. "O From this time forth my thoughts be bloody or be nothing worth." *(He "exits" to backstage.)*

MARY/OPHELIA. *(Entering with Daisy/Gertrude and Vernon/Claudius as Hamlet "exits.")* "Where is the beauteous Queen of Denmark?"

BRAUN. *(Henry and Braun again enter from opposite sides.)* Henry!

What about this? *(Showing him something inside a cardboard box.)*
HENRY. Very good. Very artistic. Show that to Gordon and see what he says.
BRAUN. No?
HENRY. No. Find the skull. Bring me the skull of Ethel Barnes Stein!
BRAUN. Gordon? Gordon, I have to talk to you. I'm sorry if I'm interrupting your preparation or your concentration or something but you know in Act Five when you have the scene with Richfield as the gravedigger and he's supposed to hand you the skull of Yorick? Well he won't because I put Yorick's skull on the prop table before half hour and checked it off like I was supposed to on the pre-show prop check list but I went back to get it to put it in the trap that's supposed to be the grave and it's gone and I've looked everywhere and Henry's going to kill me because you can't use this cantaloupe, can you? *(Taking it out of the box.)* And I'm really, really sorry but maybe you could come up with a line or something like "Methinks I held the skull of Yorick once and methought it look-ed-eth like this melon." *(He turns the cantaloupe to reveal the outlines of a skull drawn upon it in Magic Marker.)*
GORDON. Richfield, have you seen the skull?
RICHFIELD. It's in the trap.
GORDON. It's in the trap.
BRAUN. In the trap?
RICHFIELD. Put it there myself before the show. Always check your own props, my boy. When I was doing Howie with Thornton in *Our Town*, well of course all those props were imaginary but I would check 'em and set 'em just the same. Oh, and by the way, very nice work on that skull, very realistic. Every time I see it, it reminds me of someone …
BRAUN. Nobody told you? It's the skull of …
GORDON. Yes. Very nice work, Brown …
BRAUN. Braun.
GORDON. *(Hustling him off.)* Thank you, Brown. Thank you.
RICHFIELD/GRAVEDIGGER. Alright then. Where's my Second Gravedigger? Come on Susannah, old girl! *(Richfield and Susannah enter as the two Gravediggers.)* "A pickaxe and a spade, a spade / For and a shrouding sheet … "
GORDON. *(Sarah enters.)* What are you doing back here?
SARAH. No cues while Richfield does his thing with the skull of Ethel Barnes Stein. Here. Some tea. Give you a boost for Act Five.

GORDON. Do you think I need a boost?

SARAH. No. I don't think you need a boost. "How all occasions do inform against me … " was wonderful. Very emotional. You were all choked up.

GORDON. I swallowed a mosquito.

SARAH. Oh. Well, you're doing great. Don't let Vernon upstage you, though … Gordon…?

GORDON. Yeah?

SARAH. I better get back to the headset.

GORDON. Yeah. You've got cues coming up.

SARAH. Yeah. *(She starts to leave, then very deliberately returns and kisses him fully on the mouth.)* The tea was just an excuse. That's what I really wanted to do. Have a good one. *(She exits. Vernon approaches Gordon.)*

VERNON. They're listening out there.

GORDON. T.H.I. over M.F.R.

VERNON. What?

GORDON. Daisy's theory of audience involvement. Temperature-humidity index divided by the mosquito-frequency ratio.

VERNON. Yeah. Well … I just wanted to say … Well, it seems kind of OK out there.

GORDON. Yeah. It does. Thank you.

VERNON. Don't *thank* me. I just wanted to say you're doing OK. OK? And I'll be a couple of steps downstage in the last scene so you can take the stronger, the upstage position. I mean the name of the play is *Hamlet* for God's sake! See you out there.

GORDON. See you out there.

RICHFIELD/GRAVEDIGGER. *(Backing into the "wings" — ad libbing.)* "Anon, what is he that builds stronger than the carpenter? I exit-eth a moment whilst thou considerest." Gordon! The skull's not in the trap!

GORDON. Not in the trap?

RICHFIELD. *("Entering.")* "Why the grave-maker, his houses last 'til doomsday!" Ha, ha, ha!

GORDON. Daisy, where's Ethel? I mean the skull. Where's the skull?

DAISY. The skull is Ethel's?

GORDON. No. Of course not. I didn't say Ethel. I said F.L! … F.L. … "Fermenti Locus." It's Latin. The place of decay. The grave. The skull. F.L.

DAISY. You're a bit too clever for me sometimes, Gordon.

HENRY. *(Entering with the skull, giving it to Gordon.)* I found it. Under the barn.

GORDON. Richfield put it there. In the trap. That's where it was supposed to be. *(Giving it back to Henry.)*

HENRY. *(Giving it to Braun.)* Braun, put it back in the trap. *(Braun starts off.)*

TYLER. *(Tyler takes the skull from him.)* You can't put it in the trap. The scene's started.

MARY. I'll put it in the coffin. *(Mary takes the skull.)* The coffin goes in the trap.

JACK. *(Jack takes the skull.)* You can't put it in the coffin, the scene with the skull is before the scene with the coffin!

MARY. *(Taking it back.)* No, the scene with the coffin is before the scene with the skull.

VERNON. *(Taking the skull.)* No, the scene with the body is before the scene with the skull which is before the scene with the coffin.

CRAIG. *(Entering and taking the skull.)* You found Ethel! Where was she?

HENRY. Under the barn.

CRAIG. Ethel was under the barn?

DAISY. Ethel?

GORDON. F.L. "Fermenti Locus." You know, Craig, F.L.!

CRAIG. Oh. Right! F.L! … Gordon! *(He tosses the skull to Gordon.)*

GORDON. *(Giving it to Tyler.)* Tyler! Here.

TYLER. Jack, take it on with you when you enter! *(Giving it to Jack.)*

JACK. I can't take it on. Ian, sneak it out there. *(Giving it to Ian.)*

IAN. Karma, you do it! *(Giving it to Karma.)*

KARMA. No way! Here, Braun. *(Giving it to Braun.)*

BRAUN. I'll throw it over the flat.

ALL. NO! *(He places the skull on the floor to pick up the cantaloupe.)*

BRAUN. What about the cantaloupe?

ALL. NO!

JACK. Gordon, we're on.

TYLER. Gordon, here! *(Tyler and Mary both kneel simultaneously to pick up the skull. They knock heads. Hard.)*

GORDON. *("Entering.")* "Hath this fellow no feeling of his business that he sings at grave making … "

RICHFIELD/GRAVEDIGGER. *(Appearing briefly around a flat.)* "A pickaxe and a spade, a spade … " *(Ad-libbing.)* "Get me a skull! … from where it hath laid." *(Tyler hands the skull to Mary, who inadvertently gives it to Daisy.)*

DAISY. *(Beginning to recognize something familiar about that skull.)*
Ethel?

CRAIG. *(Taking the skull from Daisy.)* No. Of course not. F.L! F.L!
*(Craig tosses the skull to Henry, who throws it to Braun, to Karma, to
Ian and finally to Vernon, who places it in Richfield's hand, which has
appeared around a flat. And without missing a beat:)*

RICHFIELD/GRAVEDIGGER. "This same skull was Yorick's
skull, the King's jester … " *(He displays the skull to the "audience.")*

DAISY. The skull is Ethel's, isn't it?!

CRAIG. Yes.

DAISY. Well … she always wanted to be in *Hamlet*.

MARY. Is your head OK?

TYLER. Yeah. Is yours? *(She nods.)* Listen, what you said earlier
about maybe … about maybe falling in love … did you mean it?

MARY. Maybe. Yeah.

TYLER. Yeah? Me too. Maybe.

VERNON. Tyler, for God's sake we've got an entrance here! Get
your ass on stage!

MARY. Have a good death.

TYLER. Thanks. *(Crossing to the entrance.)* Everybody ready for
the last scene?

DAISY. Oh yes. We all get to die by poison now. Isn't that lovely?
Poison leaves so much room for acting.

TYLER/LAERTES. *("Entering" with the rest of the Company.)* "Lay
her in the earth and from her fair and unpolluted flesh let violets
spring … " *(Sound and lights indicate a passage in time to the end of
Act Five. We see the following scene as a shadow play against a back-
lit flat. Henry enters and stands out of sight lines in the wing to watch
and listen. Craig takes up a similar position on the opposite side of the
stage.)*

GORDON/HAMLET. "Here thou incestuous, murderous, damned
Dane, drink off this poison. Follow my mother."

TYLER/LAERTES. "He is justly served. Forgive me, noble Hamlet."

GORDON/HAMLET. "Heaven make thee free! I follow thee.
Horatio, I am dead; thou livst: report me and my cause aright to
the unsatisfied. O, I die, Horatio! The potent poison quite o'er-
crows my spirit I cannot live … the rest is silence."

JACK/HORATIO. "Now cracks a noble heart. Good night, sweet
prince, and flights of angels sing thee to thy rest." *(Lights fade.
Applause. Neither wild nor subdued. Appropriate. In silhouette we see*

the company take their bow as the curtain closes. Lights change. Music drifts in from an offstage party. Craig is sorting pencils. Sarah sets the ghost light.)

Scene 5

SARAH. Well, another "Auld Lang Syne" night. How many does that make for you, Craig?

CRAIG. I've stopped counting. I don't know why we all have to get up on stage in front of the audience and sing that stupid song — like we just did — closing night of every season.

SARAH. Because everybody has gotten up on stage and everybody has sung that stupid song every closing night of every season for sixty-seven years since the theatre started.

CRAIG. That's no reason.

SARAH. That's the best reason.

CRAIG. I think we could use a change.

HENRY. *(Entering.)* So do I.

SARAH. Both of you weep like babies from the first note and just because you two middle-aged cranks are embarrassed by honest sentiment is no reason to toss a sixty-seven-year-old tradition.

HENRY. You need a drink. So do I, come to think of it. *(He starts to exit.)*

SARAH. Henry! Is that…? *(Indicating the hat box we last saw bearing the mortal remains of Ethel Barnes Stein.)*

HENRY. Yes. I thought I'd take her to the closing night party.

CRAIG. Henry!

HENRY. She's my date.

SARAH. Henry!

HENRY. I haven't had a date for a number of years … nor, for that matter, has Ethel. *(He exits.)*

SARAH and CRAIG. Henry!

CRAIG. You did very well with the pencils this season, Sarah. I was very pleased with that. Efficient. It was a very efficient system.

SARAH. Efficiency in the service of art is my watchword.

CRAIG. Well, thank you, I appreciated it. *(He exits.)*

SARAH. Gordon, are you in here?

GORDON. *(Appearing from out of the shadows.)* Here. Caught me again. I just like to sit in the barn sometimes. It has a completely different feel the moment the last show has closed.

SARAH. Come on. Let's go to the party. Will you dance with me?

GORDON. I don't dance.

SARAH. We'll see about that.

JACK. *(Entering.)* Is Gordon out here?

SARAH. Yeah, he's waxing nostalgic with the mosquitoes. *(She exits.)*

JACK. I just wanted to thank you.

GORDON. No. Thank you. You did nice work this summer.

JACK. Thanks.

GORDON. Sorry about *Charley's Aunt.*

JACK. Yeah. Me too.

GORDON. It was pretty funny. I mean "funny" not funny like it was supposed to be funny. But funny like when you think about it a year from now funny.

VERNON. *(Entering.)* You want to know the really funny, funny part? You'll be dining out on stories of *Charley's Aunt* thirty years from now. People will ask you about it in actor bars and green rooms from coast to coast. It will be legendary.

GORDON. Except he'll be a lawyer and it won't be legendary in Wall Street law firms river to river. And when he tells about it they'll nod and smile but no one will understand. And pretty soon he won't tell it anymore. And after awhile he won't remember why it was funny.

VERNON. Nope. You have to be on stage to really understand. "You must be Charley's aunt?"

GORDON. *(As the gender-distressed "Fanny Babs.")* "Me? No!" *(They laugh.)*

VERNON. I've got to get my kit from the dressing room. *(Exits.)*

GORDON. So. Columbia Law? When do you start?

JACK. End of September, I guess.

GORDON. You guess?

JACK. No, I'm sure. I'm going … It's ironic though, my agent called the other day. The Guthrie Theatre wants to see me for a spot in their resident company. I told him I wasn't interested. I'm starting school.

GORDON. Right.

JACK. It might be fun to audition though. I'd probably get it now I can't do it.

GORDON. Probably.

JACK. Probably. You know, I had a thought. Columbia might defer my enrollment for a year. And it really would be nice to be a part of a company again. This summer, *Charley's Aunt* or not, has been pretty incredible. Do you think I should look into that? Deferring my enrollment? Hey, do you think there's something from Horatio I could do for my audition?

GORDON. Well, yeah, there's ummm …

JACK. *(Genuinely.)* Thanks, Gordon. Thanks for the advice. That was really helpful. And the summer. Thank you. Coming back in to the party?

GORDON. In a minute. *(Jack exits.)*

VERNON. *(Entering.)* You know if you put in air-conditioning and kept the goddamn mosquitoes out it wouldn't be so bad up here. What are you thinking for next season?

GORDON. I don't know. Haven't given it much thought what with …

VERNON. How about some Strindberg? *Dance of Death* maybe? I've always wanted to play the Captain.

SUSANNAH. *(Entering.)* Or an Ibsen … I've got a killer concept for *The Lady from the Sea.*

GORDON. Well, you know Barbara kind of has this thing about Ibsen …

SUSANNAH. Really? That is a terrific idea, Gordo, I bet she *would* sponsor it.

GORDON. Well, you know, I bet she just might. If you were the one to ask her.

SUSANNAH. She's inside at the party right now.

GORDON. Tell her it's by Henrik Ibsen, the same author as *Peer Gynt.* And be sure that she knows it was you who directed *Charley's Aunt.* That'll clinch it.

SUSANNAH. Thanks, Gordo, Thanks. *(She exits.)*

VERNON. So, what do you think? About next season.

GORDON. You'd want to come back?

VERNON. Well, I don't suppose I'll get the happy camper award, but this damn barn grows on you.

RICHFIELD. *(Entering with Daisy.)* It's the smell.

VERNON. What?

RICHFIELD. It's the smell that grows on you.

VERNON. Of the greasepaint?

RICHFIELD. Of the barn itself. Old wood. Slightly musty. Maple leaves.

DAISY. Candle smoke.

SARAH. *(Entering with two drinks.)* Mildew and bug repellent.

VERNON. Two-hundred-year-old cow sh ...

DAISY. Flop, dear. Ethel always referred to it as flop. *(Tyler and Mary enter.)* Look who's here. Where did you two come from?

RICHFIELD. I think they've been in the prop loft.

MARY. We've been checking our props! *(She cracks herself up.)*

DAISY. Oh dear, not again like *Peer Gynt*, Tyler.

MARY. Tyler...?

TYLER. Gordon, we need to ask you something.

GORDON. What?

TYLER. Well, I don't suppose it would be possible ... in fact, what with the schedule and all I'm sure it wouldn't be possible, so I won't even bother you ...

MARY. We want to know if we can get married in the barn next summer?

RICHFIELD. Oh my goodness.

DAISY. How wonderful!

SARAH. Holy shit.

DAISY. That is just wonderful. A wedding in the barn again. I can't remember the last time we had a wedding in the barn. Do you remember, Sarah?

SARAH. I think I was blacked out.

RICHFIELD. *(Changing the subject.)* Daisy ...

DAISY. I remember! It was Gordon and Sarah.

SARAH. That must be why I was blacked out.

VERNON. You two are married? I've been working with you the entire summer and I didn't know you were married?

GORDON. *Were* married.

SARAH. Not anymore.

GORDON. Divorced.

SARAH. For three years.

GORDON. Three years and four months. And nine days ...

SARAH. Gordon!? ... What about the barn?

GORDON. Sure. If you can do it before the season or on a dark night.

MARY. That is so cool. You are so cool for an old guy. Really.

TYLER. Well, only if it works with the schedule. We can't interfere with the schedule and ...

MARY. Shut up, honey. Kiss me.

SARAH. Amazing, Tyler. Only a few days ago we saw you morph into a bat and here you are morphing into a married man and that is, like wow, *really* amazing for those of us who know you.

MARY. Let's go dance.

DAISY. Yes. Let's go dance, Richfield. You too, Vernon.

VERNON. Oh God. *(They exit.)*

SARAH. You've been counting.

GORDON. Yep. *(Sarah gives him a drink.)* What's this?

SARAH. Gin and tonic. You like gin and tonic.

GORDON. *(Indicating her drink.)* What's that?

SARAH. Diet Coke. I like Diet Coke.

GORDON. *(Not judgmental.)* Really?

SARAH. Really. It's been Diet Coke all summer in fact … Mostly, anyway …

GORDON. Then why…?

SARAH. Because then I'd have to talk about it. And we'd have to talk about [us] … and I couldn't. Are you sorry you brought me back here this summer?

GORDON. No. Are you sorry you came?

SARAH. No. Can I come back next summer?

GORDON. Yes.

SARAH. Thank you … Gordon, I … *(Craig and Henry enter. Henry carries the skull.)*

CRAIG. Gordon? I think I've got some news for you. I've been toting things up …

HENRY. Closing night party and Craig is in the woodshed toting things up.

CRAIG. And I think I have all the receipts in — or at least those that aren't wadded up in the back pockets of Henry's jeans that he'll send me in December to be reimbursed but I won't because it'll be too late. And I think we are actually, remarkably, going to end the season with a small surplus.

GORDON. How much?

CRAIG. Well, I've left in a contingency, of course …

HENRY. For those wadded-up receipts in my jeans.

CRAIG. … but minus the contingency it comes out to one hundred and six dollars … which means we have no cash to start next season. So the earlier you can make your call to Mrs. DeMartineau …

HENRY. "Do, a deer, a female deer … "

GORDON. Oh God!

HENRY. We've still got the fjords, Gordon. A little touch-up and we'll make 'em Alps.

RICHFIELD. *(Entering with Daisy.)* Craig, Gordon, umh … Barbara De Martineau just …

DAISY. Yes. She certainly did.

CRAIG. What?

DAISY. Barbara deliberately dumped an entire bowl of crab and artichoke dip on Susannah's head.

CRAIG. Why on earth would she do that?

RICHFIELD. I have no idea.

SARAH. Gordon?

GORDON. I have no idea.

BRAUN. *(Entering with Karma and Ian.)* Hey, do you guys know what's going on in the farmhouse?

GORDON and SARAH. We have no idea.

MARY. *(Entering with Tyler, Jack and Vernon.)* Did you know Barbara De Martineau knows like martial arts and Susannah is a kick-boxer?

CRAIG. Who's left in there?

MARY. Just like Barbara and her friends from the country club and Susannah. But Susannah looks like way skankin' yucky …

GORDON. Shut the barn doors before they find us! *(Somebody does.)*

HENRY. And be quiet. Maybe they'll think we've all left. Shhh!

GORDON. Turn out the lights! *(Ad libs, laughter. As they all start to settle down a door bangs open. Enter Susannah, a healthy serving of crab and artichoke dip still on her head. A tense moment.)* Oh … Susannah …

HENRY. *(Drunkenly, speaking it.)* Don't you cry for me … *(Daisy motions for Susannah to sit.)*

KARMA. Wow. What an amazing end to an amazing summer!

BRAUN. Totally amazing … "Tea is served!" *(Laughter and groans from the company.)*

IAN. It was great. I think I slept maybe three hours all season.

KARMA. And I'm going to stay in touch with everybody, the whole company. You're like my family now. I am going to write and e-mail everybody all the time. We all will, I know it.

VERNON. You won't you know.

DAISY. Vernon.

VERNON. Well, she won't write everybody and everybody won't write back. You know that.

DAISY. Of course I know that. But it's "Auld Lang Syne" night and I certainly wouldn't say that.

VERNON. It's just the first job thing.

BRAUN. What do you mean? *(Vernon is about to answer …)*

SARAH. He means … that the first time you do this it is so intense that the people you work with become your entire world and it seems impossible that you won't all remain that close forever.

VERNON. But you don't.

RICHFIELD. You'll stay close to some. Bump into others from time to time at an audition ...

SARAH. But it's not the same. And you'll learn that — when you find yourself at another theatre, trying to make plays and what you really make is another little temporary family, which is, after all, what brought you into the business to begin with.

DAISY. It's why we sing the song.

KARMA. What does "Auld Lang Syne" mean, anyway?

DAISY. Well, I have always thought it means that old Mr. Lang had a sign ...

VERNON. Old Mr. Lang had a sign? Like Old MacDonald had a farm?

DAISY. Yes. Exactly. And it was a sign of ... *(Laughter and good-natured derision from the others.)* Well, it really doesn't matter. It's sweet and sad and we sing it together and I love the way Sarah takes the harmony at the end and ...

RICHFIELD. And it's about old acquaintance ...

TYLER. And friendship ...

SARAH. And not forgetting ...

GORDON. And telling stories in a barn on a summer night.

HENRY. *(Drunkenly, quietly begins. They all join in raggedly. At the last line, they blend in an achingly sweet harmony, each lost in their own world. Sarah takes Gordon's hand. Lights fade.)*

> Should old acquaintance be forgot and never brought to mind
> Should old acquaintance be forgot and days of auld lang syne.
> For auld lang syne, my dear, for auld lang syne,
> We'll take a cup of kindness yet for days of auld lang syne.

End of Play

PROPERTY LIST

Scripts
Various notes, handouts, pieces of paper
Flashlight (GORDON)
Matches (GORDON)
Bag (MARY)
Briefcase (VERNON)
Cell phone (GORDON)
Drinking glasses (VERNON, SARAH)
Hat box (HENRY, GORDON)
Tea service (BRAUN)
Hat (RICHFIELD)
Coca-Cola products (CRAIG)
Long roll of fabric (HENRY)
Stub of a pencil (HENRY)
Ladder (KARMA, IAN, BRAUN)
Crucifix (KARMA, RICHFIELD, JACK, VERNON)
Coins (JACK)
Eye drops (JACK)
Newspaper (VERNON)
Diary (MARY)
Lighting instrument (MARY)
Crowbar (VERNON)
Mallet (KARMA)
Stake (KARMA)
Textbook (JACK)
Cardboard box containing a cantaloupe (BRAUN)
Skull (HENRY)
Ice pack (MARY, TYLER)
Pencils (CRAIG)

SOUND EFFECTS

Spooky music
Wolf howling
Sound of tape rewinding
Sound of door creaking open and shut
Gunshot
Dogs barking
Music playing at wrong speed
Sounds of a party
Audience laughing
Audience clapping

NEW PLAYS

★ **MOTHERHOOD OUT LOUD by Leslie Ayvazian, Brooke Berman, David Cale, Jessica Goldberg, Beth Henley, Lameece Issaq, Claire LaZebnik, Lisa Loomer, Michele Lowe, Marco Pennette, Theresa Rebeck, Luanne Rice, Annie Weisman and Cheryl L. West, conceived by Susan R. Rose and Joan Stein.** When entrusting the subject of motherhood to such a dazzling collection of celebrated American writers, what results is a joyous, moving, hilarious, and altogether thrilling theatrical event. "Never fails to strike both the funny bone and the heart." *–BackStage.* "Packed with wisdom, laughter, and plenty of wry surprises." *–TheaterMania.* [1M, 3W] ISBN: 978-0-8222-2589-8

★ **COCK by Mike Bartlett.** When John takes a break from his boyfriend, he accidentally meets the girl of his dreams. Filled with guilt and indecision, he decides there is only one way to straighten this out. "[A] brilliant and blackly hilarious feat of provocation." *–Independent.* "A smart, prickly and rewarding view of sexual and emotional confusion." *–Evening Standard.* [3M, 1W] ISBN: 978-0-8222-2766-3

★ **F. Scott Fitzgerald's THE GREAT GATSBY adapted for the stage by Simon Levy.** Jay Gatsby, a self-made millionaire, passionately pursues the elusive Daisy Buchanan. Nick Carraway, a young newcomer to Long Island, is drawn into their world of obsession, greed and danger. "Levy's combination of narration, dialogue and action delivers most of what is best in the novel." *–Seattle Post-Intelligencer.* "A beautifully crafted interpretation of the 1925 novel which defined the Jazz Age." *–London Free Press.* [5M, 4W] ISBN: 978-0-8222-2727-4

★ **LONELY, I'M NOT by Paul Weitz.** At an age when most people are discovering what they want to do with their lives, Porter has been married and divorced, earned seven figures as a corporate "ninja," and had a nervous breakdown. It's been four years since he's had a job or a date, and he's decided to give life another shot. "Critic's pick!" *–NY Times.* "An enjoyable ride." *–NY Daily News.* [3M, 3W] ISBN: 978-0-8222-2734-2

★ **ASUNCION by Jesse Eisenberg.** Edgar and Vinny are not racist. In fact, Edgar maintains a blog condemning American imperialism, and Vinny is three-quarters into a Ph.D. in Black Studies. When Asuncion becomes their new roommate, the boys have a perfect opportunity to demonstrate how open-minded they truly are. "Mr. Eisenberg writes lively dialogue that strikes plenty of comic sparks." *–NY Times.* "An almost ridiculously enjoyable portrait of slacker trauma among would-be intellectuals." *–Newsday.* [2M, 2W] ISBN: 978-0-8222-2630-7

DRAMATISTS PLAY SERVICE, INC.
440 Park Avenue South, New York, NY 10016 212-683-8960 Fax 212-213-1539
postmaster@dramatists.com www.dramatists.com

NEW PLAYS

★ **THE PICTURE OF DORIAN GRAY by Roberto Aguirre-Sacasa, based on the novel by Oscar Wilde.** Preternaturally handsome Dorian Gray has his portrait painted by his college classmate Basil Hallwood. When their mutual friend Henry Wotton offers to include it in a show, Dorian makes a fateful wish—that his portrait should grow old instead of him—and strikes an unspeakable bargain with the devil. [5M, 2W] ISBN: 978-0-8222-2590-4

★ **THE LYONS by Nicky Silver.** As Ben Lyons lies dying, it becomes clear that he and his wife have been at war for many years, and his impending demise has brought no relief. When they're joined by their children all efforts at a sentimental goodbye to the dying patriarch are soon abandoned. "Hilariously frank, clear-sighted, compassionate and forgiving." *–NY Times.* "Mordant, dark and rich." *–Associated Press.* [3M, 3W] ISBN: 978-0-8222-2659-8

★ **STANDING ON CEREMONY by Mo Gaffney, Jordan Harrison, Moisés Kaufman, Neil LaBute, Wendy MacLeod, José Rivera, Paul Rudnick, and Doug Wright, conceived by Brian Shnipper.** Witty, warm and occasionally wacky, these plays are vows to the blessings of equality, the universal challenges of relationships and the often hilarious power of love. "CEREMONY puts a human face on a hot-button issue and delivers laughter and tears rather than propaganda." *–BackStage.* [3M, 3W] ISBN: 978-0-8222-2654-3

★ **ONE ARM by Moisés Kaufman, based on the short story and screenplay by Tennessee Williams.** Ollie joins the Navy and becomes the lightweight boxing champion of the Pacific Fleet. Soon after, he loses his arm in a car accident, and he turns to hustling to survive. "[A] fast, fierce, brutally beautiful stage adaptation." *–NY Magazine.* "A fascinatingly lurid, provocative and fatalistic piece of theater." *–Variety.* [7M, 1W] ISBN: 978-0-8222-2564-5

★ **AN ILIAD by Lisa Peterson and Denis O'Hare.** A modern-day retelling of Homer's classic. Poetry and humor, the ancient tale of the Trojan War and the modern world collide in this captivating theatrical experience. "Shocking, glorious, primal and deeply satisfying." *–Time Out NY.* "Explosive, altogether breathtaking." *–Chicago Sun-Times.* [1M] ISBN: 978-0-8222-2687-1

★ **THE COLUMNIST by David Auburn.** At the height of the Cold War, Joe Alsop is the nation's most influential journalist, beloved, feared and courted by the Washington world. But as the '60s dawn and America undergoes dizzying change, the intense political dramas Joe is embroiled in become deeply personal as well. "Intensely satisfying." *–Bloomberg News.* [5M, 2W] ISBN: 978-0-8222-2699-4

DRAMATISTS PLAY SERVICE, INC.
440 Park Avenue South, New York, NY 10016 212-683-8960 Fax 212-213-1539
postmaster@dramatists.com www.dramatists.com

NEW PLAYS

★ **BENGAL TIGER AT THE BAGHDAD ZOO by Rajiv Joseph.** The lives of two American Marines and an Iraqi translator are forever changed by an encounter with a quick-witted tiger who haunts the streets of war-torn Baghdad. "[A] boldly imagined, harrowing and surprisingly funny drama." *–NY Times.* "Tragic yet darkly comic and highly imaginative." *–CurtainUp.* [5M, 2W] ISBN: 978-0-8222-2565-2

★ **THE PITMEN PAINTERS by Lee Hall, inspired by a book by William Feaver.** Based on the triumphant true story, a group of British miners discover a new way to express themselves and unexpectedly become art-world sensations. "Excitingly ambiguous, in-the-moment theater." *–NY Times.* "Heartfelt, moving and deeply politicized." *–Chicago Tribune.* [5M, 2W] ISBN: 978-0-8222-2507-2

★ **RELATIVELY SPEAKING by Ethan Coen, Elaine May and Woody Allen.** In TALKING CURE, Ethan Coen uncovers the sort of insanity that can only come from family. Elaine May explores the hilarity of passing in GEORGE IS DEAD. In HONEYMOON MOTEL, Woody Allen invites you to the sort of wedding day you won't forget. "Firecracker funny." *–NY Times.* "A rollicking good time." *–New Yorker.* [8M, 7W] ISBN: 978-0-8222-2394-8

★ **SONS OF THE PROPHET by Stephen Karam.** If to live is to suffer, then Joseph Douaihy is more alive than most. With unexplained chronic pain and the fate of his reeling family on his shoulders, Joseph's health, sanity, and insurance premium are on the line. "Explosively funny." *–NY Times.* "At once deep, deft and beautifully made." *–New Yorker.* [5M, 3W] ISBN: 978-0-8222-2597-3

★ **THE MOUNTAINTOP by Katori Hall.** A gripping reimagination of events the night before the assassination of the civil rights leader Dr. Martin Luther King, Jr. "An ominous electricity crackles through the opening moments." *–NY Times.* "[A] thrilling, wild, provocative flight of magical realism." *–Associated Press.* "Crackles with theatricality and a humanity more moving than sainthood." *–NY Newsday.* [1M, 1W] ISBN: 978-0-8222-2603-1

★ **ALL NEW PEOPLE by Zach Braff.** Charlie is 35, heartbroken, and just wants some time away from the rest of the world. Long Beach Island seems to be the perfect escape until his solitude is interrupted by a motley parade of misfits who show up and change his plans. "Consistently and sometimes sensationally funny." *–NY Times.* "A morbidly funny play about the trendy new existential condition of being young, adorable, and miserable." *–Variety.* [2M, 2W] ISBN: 978-0-8222-2562-1

DRAMATISTS PLAY SERVICE, INC.
440 Park Avenue South, New York, NY 10016 212-683-8960 Fax 212-213-1539
postmaster@dramatists.com   www.dramatists.com

NEW PLAYS

★ **CLYBOURNE PARK by Bruce Norris.** WINNER OF THE 2011 PULITZER PRIZE AND 2012 TONY AWARD. Act One takes place in 1959 as community leaders try to stop the sale of a home to a black family. Act Two is set in the same house in the present day as the now predominantly African-American neighborhood battles to hold its ground. "Vital, sharp-witted and ferociously smart." –*NY Times*. "A theatrical treasure…Indisputably, uproariously funny." –*Entertainment Weekly*. [4M, 3W] ISBN: 978-0-8222-2697-0

★ **WATER BY THE SPOONFUL by Quiara Alegría Hudes.** WINNER OF THE 2012 PULITZER PRIZE. A Puerto Rican veteran is surrounded by the North Philadelphia demons he tried to escape in the service. "This is a very funny, warm, and yes uplifting play." –*Hartford Courant*. "The play is a combination poem, prayer and app on how to cope in an age of uncertainty, speed and chaos." –*Variety*. [4M, 3W] ISBN: 978-0-8222-2716-8

★ **RED by John Logan.** WINNER OF THE 2010 TONY AWARD. Mark Rothko has just landed the biggest commission in the history of modern art. But when his young assistant, Ken, gains the confidence to challenge him, Rothko faces the agonizing possibility that his crowning achievement could also become his undoing. "Intense and exciting." –*NY Times*. "Smart, eloquent entertainment." –*New Yorker*. [2M] ISBN: 978-0-8222-2483-9

★ **VENUS IN FUR by David Ives.** Thomas, a beleaguered playwright/director, is desperate to find an actress to play Vanda, the female lead in his adaptation of the classic sadomasochistic tale *Venus in Fur*. "Ninety minutes of good, kinky fun." –*NY Times*. "A fast-paced journey into one man's entrapment by a clever, vengeful female." –*Associated Press*. [1M, 1W] ISBN: 978-0-8222-2603-1

★ **OTHER DESERT CITIES by Jon Robin Baitz.** Brooke returns home to Palm Springs after a six-year absence and announces that she is about to publish a memoir dredging up a pivotal and tragic event in the family's history—a wound they don't want reopened. "Leaves you feeling both moved and gratifyingly sated." –*NY Times*. "A genuine pleasure." –*NY Post*. [2M, 3W] ISBN: 978-0-8222-2605-5

★ **TRIBES by Nina Raine.** Billy was born deaf into a hearing family and adapts brilliantly to his family's unconventional ways, but it's not until he meets Sylvia, a young woman on the brink of deafness, that he finally understands what it means to be understood. "A smart, lively play." –*NY Times*. "[A] bright and boldly provocative drama." –*Associated Press*. [3M, 2W] ISBN: 978-0-8222-2751-9

DRAMATISTS PLAY SERVICE, INC.
440 Park Avenue South, New York, NY 10016 212-683-8960 Fax 212-213-1539
postmaster@dramatists.com www.dramatists.com